There is great authority in these straightforward truths to propel us to the same life-style as well. Thank you, Ron, for putting in words the things that are in our hearts and for living your life in such a way that we believe that we can do it too. —*Jimmy Seibert, Senior Pastor, Antioch Community Church and Director of Antioch Ministries International, Waco, Texas*

Ron Parrish's new book on prayer is so refreshing and practical. From the youngest believer to the most mature, this book has something for everyone. You too can find prayer to be a delight.

—*Larry Kreider, International Director, DOVE Christian Fellowship International, Lititz, Pennsylvania*

From Duty to Delight is not just a book title for Ron Parrish. It is his life. I served together with Ron at Church in the City in Houston, and have observed his life for close to thirty years. He has always delighted in prayer and challenged me to do the same. Reading *From Duty to Delight* was a delight. The book is warm, personal and inviting. Reading it was like drinking a cup of hot cappuccino at Starbucks with a friend, while he warmed my heart to pray more and better. I strongly recommend this practical, non-religious, guide for *turning daily prayer from ought-to to want-to*. It will refresh the experienced prayer, and provide an excellent tool for establishing prayer as a way of life for new disciples.

—*Berten Waggoner, National Director, Vineyard Churches, USA*

From Duty To Delight

Nancy,
May you experience
greater intimacy in your
times of prayer through applying
some of the insights of this book.

Tom Farrel

From Duty To Delight
Finding Greater Joy in Daily Prayer

Partnership
Publications

A Division of House to House Publications

From Duty To Delight: Finding Greater Joy in Daily Prayer

Copyright © 2006 by Ron Parrish
4407 Monterey Oaks Blvd. Suite 120
Austin, Texas 78754
All rights reserved

ISBN 0-9778614-1-4

Partnership Publications
A Division of House to House Publications
www.H2HP.com

Unless otherwise noted, all scripture quotations in this publication are taken from the Holy Bible, New International Version (NIV). © 1973, 1978, 1984 by International Bible Society. Used by permission of Zondervan Publishing House. All rights reserved.

Printed in the United States of America

Cover design: William Hollis

Contents

Acknowledgments

When the idea of writing this book began rattling around in my head in October of 2004, I knew I would need some confirmation that this project was really from God. I also knew I would desperately need some help. Confirmation came from some precious Indonesian church leaders whom I had invested in during the decade of the 80's. Conversations with my friends Paulus, Salmon, Lilik, Gatot, Yakolina, and Pak Rumkeney inspired me to put into writing some of the things that I had taught and modeled during our time in Indonesia. The words of my friend Jeff Hartensveld were humbling but kept reverberating in my soul and pushed me to *go for it* when I often thought: "What do I have to contribute here?" He said: "Ron, the legacy you left behind for the missionary community in Indonesia was your devotional life."

Help came from a number of sources. My friend Mike O'Quin was my editor and also a major source of encouragement. Jonelle Tucker corrected a ton of my grammar and spelling mistakes. Billie Hollis created (and recreated) the cover design. Sarah Sauder from House to House/Partnership Publications has been my biggest cheerleader. I had been told by several experienced writers that publishers can be difficult to work with so plan on self-publishing. My experience has been the opposite. Sarah and people at Partnership Publications have championed this project since they first read the manuscript. I am truly honored by their support.

Finally, I owe a debt of gratitude to the congregation and pastoral leadership team at Hope in the City. They love me, honor me, and affirm me way beyond what I deserve. I've learned so much about prayer through hours spent seeking the Lord with them during these last six years.

—Ron Parrish, Austin, Texas, May 2006

Foreword

The best things in life are transferred from one person to another, life on life, heart to heart. If you want to learn something from someone, spend time with a person who knows what they are talking about.

If you want to learn to pray, listen to those who love to spend time with God. Get close to them, pray with them, join them as they usher you into God's presence. Be encouraged by their faith and by their zeal. Catch their heart for being alone with God.

Ron does that for us in this book. What he really does is invite us to get close to his heart, to spend time alone with him as he opens his soul to God. *From Duty to Delight* is more than a book. Think of it as an opportunity to be mentored by a man who loves to encourage, accepts people readily, and has a contagious relationship with God.

Without being religious or condemning, Ron shares his passion for prayer He is fervent without being pushy. He motivates others to pray because he loves to pray, not because he likes to make people feel guilty. Ron doesn't see prayer as a duty to perform, but an invitation to receive life.

From Duty to Delight is also very practical. Ron understands that spending time alone with God involves variety and creativity, just as spending time with friends involves the same thing. Very few people on the planet would enjoy a relationship with another person that involved sitting quietly with the other person, each with their eyes closed, talking quietly for hours on end. No change, same routine, every day, same place. Sound boring? It is boring.

Ron approaches prayer knowing that it is much more than one-dimensional exercise. He offers a wealth of tools to aid you in your times alone with God. He teaches the reader ways of praying and spending time alone with God that will release creativity and joy in their friendship with God.

Ron is a student of human nature. He knows people. He actually likes people. He knows that each person is unique in how they relate to God. At the same time that he accepts people, Ron also realizes that for payer to have meaning it has be God-centered and full of substance. There is depth in this book because there is depth in Ron Parrish's relationship with God.

I have waited a long time for this book. I recommend it with confidence. I will use it to mentor those who are just learning to pray, and to encourage those who are already on the journey.

—Floyd McClung, Director, All Nations

Introduction

You're probably like me; too many books, so little time. I've got to be convinced of a book's relevance to my felt needs. I appreciate it when a person tells me what they are about to tell me so I'll know if I want to or *need to* take note of what they are saying. So I'll be upfront with you. This book is *not* for you if you are satisfied with your devotional life. It's written for the average non-prayer-warrior who struggles to set aside time daily for a meaningful, focused interaction with God. It will be worth the read if you are like my friend Bill who confides in me that he ...

- is hit or miss in his personal devotions and feels bad about it.
- quickly runs out of things to say when he tries to pray.
- finds prayer to be, quite frankly, boring at times.
- has given up on trying to be a "man of prayer."

The purpose of this book is to help you find joy in the discipline of daily prayer. It's written to inspire you, motivate you, and give you some practical help in experiencing a life-style of meaningful interaction with God. It's not about how many chapters in the Bible you read or about how many minutes a day you pray. It's about becoming a person who really enjoys spending time in God's presence—so much so that you lose track of time. My desire is to turn prayer from an *ought-to* into a *want-to* for you.

In the self-help section of our local *Barnes and Nobles* bookstore I've counted dozens of titles that suggest how middle-aged guys like me can get in shape. Consider this as a workbook on developing a spiritual fitness workout regimen. The goal is simple: to become strong in *Spirit*. Many books inspire me to love and live for God. Few books offer me practical training in how to embrace spirituality in a practical, every-day dialogue with God. The Word says: *Spend your time and energy in training yourself for spiritual fitness. Physical exercise has some value, but spiritual exercise is much more important, for it promises a reward in both this life and the next.*[1]

One really learns prayer by *doing prayer*. This book will be most helpful to you if you stretch your prayer muscles by experimenting with the various *kinds of prayer*[2] suggested. At the end of each chapter you will be given a *Prayer Lab*. Try out the lab experiments, reflect on them, and then try to discuss them with a friend.

On a personal note, it took some convincing for me to write this book. I've never aspired to be an author (I can't even type!). I launched into this project after a trip to Indonesia in 2004. Janine and I had served there as missionaries from 1983 to 1992. We had the indescribable privilege of planting churches and training church planters among a responsive Muslim people group on the island of Java. On this recent trip, I happened to connect with a number of my former disciples/students who are now teaching in seminaries, pastoring churches, and leading church planting movements. Each of them expressed appreciation for the way I had helped in their spiritual formation through modeling and teaching prayer. They lovingly persuaded me to put into writing some of the things I'm learning about prayer. (My hope is that this book will be soon translated into Indonesian.)

My prayer is for your prayer life. I want you to find a richness and intimacy with God that you have never experienced before. I want you to touch His heart every day, to feel His immense love for you, and to be overwhelmed by His goodness to you. I want you to submit to God and resist the devil. I want you to fight for your family. I want you to experience *life* in your prayer times.

Chapter 1

Motivations: Desperation and Expectation

He who has learned to pray has learned the greatest secret of a holy and happy life. —William Law

"My prayer life is really lame. I find myself talking a lot *about* God but taking so little time to talk *with* Him lately." This sentiment was expressed to me recently by a friend who happens to serve as the senior pastor of a very large church. It seems that most Christians I know, even Christian leaders, are dissatisfied with their personal intimacy with the Lord.

When I ask people: "What's the greatest challenge you face in carving out time to pray?" I usually get answers like: "The demands of my job," "My hectic schedule in the morning," "Getting the kids off to school," "My commute to work," or "I don't get enough sleep as it is...." Most people feel that they are too busy and just don't have time to pray.

But "I'm too busy to pray" translates as: "Of all the demands on my time, prayer is expendable." The problem is motivation more than busyness. When we are highly motivated to do something, we get it done. Heart precedes action. You will make time for that which you value. It's that simple. Avid football fans don't need to be told to carve out time to watch their favorite team play on the weekend. Hearty, happy eaters don't need to be told: "You really need to make time to eat for your body to get the nutrition that comes from eating enough." They already have *intrinsic motivation*.

Motivation is the key

When I was a young disciple, I caught on early that I was supposed to pray. I heard that Christians need to pray and read their Bibles every day. I really did love Jesus, but having a consistent and meaningful time of prayer was elusive. I made numerous commitments to pray—while at youth camp, on mission trips, and other times that I felt an overwhelming zeal to try to be a praying Christian. How quickly the desire to pray would wane. I usually failed to pray more than two or three days in a row. Worse, these prayer times were not that fun or fulfilling. I quickly fell into an empty ritual of "religious activity" that was far from relational. I found that obligation, guilt, or even a *commitment to pray* didn't sustain a meaningful prayer life.

There were some other motivations in those early years that didn't really work for me (Trust me; I tried them.):

- Performance (I'd better get it together in my devotional life to gain God's approval.)
- Penitence or "sin tax" (I've blown it so I had better pray in order to *pay for* my sin.)
- Fear (I'd better pray so nothing bad will happen to me.)
- Comparison (If I really want to become a great man of God like Martin Luther, John Wesley, or Billy Graham, I'd better pray more.)

In the midst of this empty obligation and guilt-based motivation, I one day came across this statement in Luke: *Yet the news about him spread all the more, so that crowds of people came to hear him and to be healed of their sicknesses. But Jesus often withdrew to lonely places and prayed.*[1] I started to ask myself: "What motivated Jesus to pray? Why did Jesus pull away from the most important, meaningful tasks that anyone could possibly be doing in order to be alone with God (healing the sick and preaching the Good News of the kingdom of God)?" I felt that if I could discover and embrace those motivations, I would more freely set aside the tasks of my day in order to prioritize time with God. I would really value prayer more—and my fuel for this would be intrinsic motivation. For more than twenty-five years I've been on a spiritual journey of discovering His motivations and letting those become my own.

Motivations That Keep Me Wanting to Spend Time With God on a Daily Basis:

I am desperate

Jesus was deeply dependent on the Father for everything. Jesus gave them this answer: *"I tell you the truth, the Son can do nothing by himself; he can do only what he sees his Father doing, because whatever the Father does the Son also does."*[2] Jesus was motivated to withdraw to lonely places and pray because He knew He needed God's help. He had to hear from God in order to say what the Father was saying.[3] He needed to spend focused time with the Father in order to learn to do what the Father was doing.

Let me state the obvious: If Jesus the son of God was desperate for the Father's help, *how much more are you and I!* My woeful inadequacy will always sabotage my ability to live the life I want to live. I more than need God's help. Name any area of my life and I can make a strong case for my own incompetence. I'm desperately dependent on God if I'm to be the kind of father, husband, friend, neighbor, pastor, or leader that God has called me to be.

If you feel desperate enough to pray, you're in good company. Mother Teresa was driven to pray with this sense of need: "I don't think there is anyone who needs God's help and grace as much as I do. Sometimes I feel so helpless and weak. I think that's why God uses me. Because I cannot depend on my own strength, I rely on Him twenty-four hours a day. If the day had even more hours, then I would need His grace and His help in those hours as well."[4]

Prayer is the ultimate expression of humility. If we feel competent to handle life without God, who needs to pray? Our prayer life shows just how desperate we are. Could it be that our prayerlessness is a reflection of the pride of our hearts?

Or maybe the goals we have for our lives are way too small and manageable so as to not need God. Our prayerlessness could point to a life of low expectations. A few "God help me's" are tossed to heaven on your rush hour commute because you are living in survival mode instead of an expectation of abundant life.

In the summer of 2004 I pursued a dream that had been on my heart for years. I spent a month on a remote island in Indonesia where there were very few Christians. Pairing up with different co-workers I knew, we drove around this beautiful island on motorcycles and asked God to use our time there. We had one goal—to plant a church! This was a simple goal, but impossible for us to accomplish without God's miraculous help. The strategy was to:

1. Engage as many Muslims as possible in conversations where we shared the gospel.
2. Pray for anyone who expressed a need, with the hopes that God would demonstrate the power of His kingdom to meet those needs.
3. Find the "man of peace" (see Luke 10) who would respond to the Good News and then become the catalyst for a new church.

It was not difficult to feel the need to spend huge chunks of time in prayer during that month. We were desperate! It was a terrible, yet wonderful feeling. God seems most ready to meet you and me when we are utterly and totally helpless, yet looking to Him to save us! At the end of the month when we boarded the ferry leaving that island, we believed God had begun to answer our prayers. (I'll share more of the details in Chapter 12.)

How could one seriously heed the Apostle Paul's admonition: *And pray in the Spirit on all occasions with all kinds of prayers and requests.*[5] Or even more challenging: *Pray continually.*[6] One way to want to pray a lot is to really believe that prayer *is* necessary on *all occasions.* I once heard about a man who went from a life-style of rarely praying to praying 6-8 hours a day. He was a pilot who was shot down over Vietnam. Colonel Robbie Reisner went through the horrendous ordeal of being imprisoned in North Vietnam in the "Hanoi Hilton" for 2,706 days. He learned to pray to survive. His courageous example inspired other POWs. If we could see ourselves that needy, that dependent on prayer and if we could visualize ourselves in desperate straits, behind enemy lines, I'm convinced it would be easier to prioritize prayer.

I have a growing expectation in the power of prayer to affect change

A lot of people look at prayer as a religious nicety, a little piece of garnish on the full plate of their lives. Prayer seems about as life-changing as tweezing your eyebrow hairs. It's the right thing to do, like flossing, but it's not that powerful or potent.

Jesus prayed because, not only did He "need" to pray, He knew His prayers made a difference. *While Jesus was here on earth, he offered prayers and pleadings, with a loud cry and tears, to the one who could deliver him out of death. And God heard His prayers because of his reverence for God.*[7]

Jesus believed that His interaction with the Father affected change. He walked in authority to chase out demons and heal the sick as the result of being with the Father daily. He lived in a confident expectation that His Father was always at work, answering His prayers. *Father, thank you for hearing me. You always hear me....* [8]

Imagine a day with Jesus. He gets up early to spend time with the Father. You see Him in the distance, taking a walk by Himself and crying out to God. Later in the day you marvel at how a beggar got up and danced after his lame legs were totally healed. You hear demons shrieking in fear as he casts them out of a demonized woman.

Perhaps the real "work of the kingdom" happened in those early morning hours when Jesus was alone with God the Father. The powers of the evil one were conquered in prayer. During the remainder of the day as He encountered hurting, lost, demonized people and set them free, Jesus was experiencing the outcome of what had already transpired in prayer. He stayed connected with the Father all day, but what happened in those early hours was critical in Jesus kingdom work.

If you and I can see our prayers as *powerful and effective*[9] as Jesus did, wouldn't we want to pray more?

Even if I believed my time with the Lord was only an activity that keeps me spiritually fit—like a heavenly workout—there would be some motivation to pray. But prayer is so much more than that. When you and I pray, we affect the future. John Wesley said, "Nothing happens except through prayer." I don't fully understand this truth, but I know through my asking, spiritual power is released and what I bind or loose in heaven is bound or loosed on earth.[10] Moses prayed and God spared the people of Israel.[11] The early church prayed and Peter was released from prison.[12] *The earnest prayer of a righteous person has great power and wonderful results.*[13]

George Mueller was known as an outstanding Christian humanitarian through the orphanages that he founded in Bristol,

England, in the 19ᵗʰ century. He led and served orphanages there for 60 years, and the legacy he left behind was immeasurable. Tens of thousands of children were clothed, nurtured, fed and led to a saving knowledge of Jesus Christ through his influence. On many occasions Mueller would be told that there was not enough food for the next meal at the orphanage. His biography notes miraculous provision, often in the eleventh hour. Never did the children miss a meal or go without clothing. His faith to believe God to provide for all of the financial needs of his ministry has inspired countless believers to follow His example of dependent faith. His journals record more than 30,000 answers to prayer!

The prayer journals I've kept for the last three decades contain some amazing testimonies of answered prayer (not quite 30,000 yet!). I've written out thousands of requests for:

- Healing for myself and others
- Financial provision
- Jobs
- Marriages to be restored
- Lost people to hear and believe the gospel
- People to be released from prison
- Childless couples to conceive and give birth to healthy children
- Kids to get accepted into college
- And numerous other random (yet specific) longings of my heart

I've made it a point to record the date I start praying for something and the date the prayer is answered. I am very aware that any miraculous answer to these prayers is solely because of the grace and mercy of God. On many occasions I was joining the prayers of others. Some of the petitions I've recorded have gone unanswered, yet I feel motivated to keep on asking. I've just seen God answer too many prayers to stop! The "effectiveness" of prayer motivates me to *go for it*.

You can confidently ask God to answer your prayers because He is glorified through answered prayer. *And I will do whatever you ask in my name, so that the Son may bring glory to the Father.*[14]

Prayer lab

THIS WEEK Sit down with a trusted friend or your spouse and answer these questions:

1. How would you describe your prayer life like right now?

2. What are the biggest challenges you face in setting aside a consistent, satisfying amount of time to really connect with God?

3. Spend some time telling God how you would answer questions 1 and 2.

Chapter 2

Motivations: Delight and Awareness

Discovering the right motivations to pray is the key to cultivating a life-style of intimacy with God through daily prayer. In
the last chapter we focused on two reasons to pray: desperation
and a growing confidence that prayer affects change.

There are two more motivations that get me out of bed in time
to pray each day.

I find a growing delight in being in the presence of God

Jesus was delighted to spend time with the Father. He made
time to withdraw from the crowds because of His deep affection
for His Father. Their relationship was characterized by intimate
love. Jesus came to earth having been together with the Father
since before the creation of the world. When He got up early after
a short night of rest and slipped away to a quiet place, He was
drawn by love. One hallmark of people in love is they can't get
enough of spending time together.

When Janine and I were dating, no one needed to tell me to
spend more time with my girlfriend. We lived on opposite sides of
the city, but we made it a priority to hang out if at all possible
(before *hanging out* was the vernacular). If for some reason we
didn't get to see each other on campus, we talked by phone. I can't
remember all we said in those countless hours with the telephone

glued to our ears. I do remember it was easy making those conversations a priority in my day. We were in love (and still are). When asked what the *secret* was to her devotion to God even Mother Teresa answered, "My secret is simple: I pray. Through prayer I become one with Christ. I realize that prayer to Him is loving Him."

Our family played a game once that asked this question: "If you had an hour with a person from history whom you most admire, who would it be?" Duh! Jesus Christ comes to mind for most of us. And we get to spend time with Him any time we make time! No one knows us better yet still loves us in spite of our weaknesses and failures, our self-centeredness and inconsistencies.

You and I can want to spend time with God because we love being with Him. His love can capture our affections. We can say with David, *you fill me with joy in your presence, with eternal pleasures at your right hand.*[1] Our love for God can become so tangible and so intense that we would rather be with Him than at the best party in town. His love can become *more delightful than wine.*[2] Prayer is meant to be *enjoyed.* Some of you know what it's like when you feel God's love for you—touching your heart, healing your wounds, affirming you in your insecurities, relieving you of your stress, giving a peace that the world cannot give.[3] Why would we want to let anything crowd out that privilege we can enjoy of experiencing God's presence?

Here's a simple test to reveal how much this love-motivation has affected you: How much time do you spend seeking the presence of God when you have a day off? When there are no pressing demands on your day, do you deliberately set aside more time to "hang out" with the Father? How about on vacation?

Can you imagine a pattern of living in which…
* you would rather pray than watch TV, eat, or go to a movie?
* prayer is so much *fun* you actually pray more when you have more discretionary time?
* you are so satisfied being in the presence of God you wouldn't have to find comfort in the empty, mindless addictions that we tend to turn to?

I can.

I have an increasing awareness of how much God delights in my presence

Jesus was so aware of the Father's love for Him. He knew the Father's approval.[4] He reveled in His Father's affections for Him.[5] Undoubtedly knowing that God was eagerly waiting to meet with Him in that place of solitude kept Jesus coming back.

This one has been more difficult for me to grasp—that God actually enjoys my presence. Intellectually, I can affirm that the Bible teaches God's loves for us. I can know with my head that: *He will take great delight in you, he will quiet you with his love, he will rejoice over you with singing.*[6] It's a challenge for my heart to accept this so I need help. The Holy Spirit helps us know (in the Hebraic sense—relationally) and experience God's Father-love for us. *God has poured out his love in our hearts **by the Holy Spirit.***[7]

Numerous encounters with the Holy Spirit in the course of my spiritual journey have helped me begin to grasp *how wide and long and high and deep is* God's proactive, fatherly, unconditional love for me.[8] This became so real to me when I was in prayer one day. I happened to be on a two-week trip into the jungles of Irian Jaya (now called Western Papua). While praying during my regular time in the morning, I had a strong impression that I was being bear-hugged by a huge, giant of a man. It wasn't painful. Just the opposite: I felt so loved. It dawned on me that this big burly "guy" was God! I couldn't see his face. My face was buried in his chest. My first response was to try to push back. I immediately thought of several reasons why I did not deserve this expression of love. I felt so unworthy. He wouldn't release me from his grasp. I sobbed as waves and waves of liquid love flowed from Him to me. I then wanted to fall on my knees and worship. "Not now," He said. I don't know how long this lasted. What I do know is my prayer life soared to a new level. Tears still come to my eyes as I recount that revelation of God's love. As I came back to earth, I had the distinct impression that God wants to reveal His love to me far more often than I am willing to accept it.

Another way I'm beginning to understand the depth of God's love for me is through how much I enjoy being with my children. They are grown and away from home, but I find myself delighted at the news that they are coming over. Connecting with them is really important to me. A lunch appointment with Heather makes my day. I read and reread emails from my daughter Misi when she was living in Irian Jaya. I get excited when Bowen and I make plans for a hunting or fishing trip—just the two of us. I love it when we have time together. When we are apart I miss them desperately. I believe God loves me and longs to be with me even more than I love being with my children.

Imagine how much easier it would be to crawl out of bed thirty minutes earlier if you were convinced that God was eager to meet with you.

Imagine Him waiting, next to your bed, eagerly anticipating the moment you open your eyes. He has so much love to share with you. He is actually waiting to hear from you—to hear about your struggles, joys, fears and sorrows. He's wanting to speak to you, counsel you, tell you of His great affection for you. He is wanting to connect with you on a heart level. He is doing everything He can to woo you into a love relationship That's more tangible, more authentic than the most intense father-son or father-daughter relationship you've ever dreamed about. He's doing all He can to demonstrate His affections for you. I believe the more you experience His love, the more you will want to pray.

Prayer Lab

1. Do you find yourself praying more when you have discretionary time? Why/why not?

2. Of the four motivations that Ron mentioned, which motivates you to want to pray more?

3. Ask God for a fresh revelation of His love for you today.

Chapter 3

Making Time for Prayer

They devoted themselves to… prayer.[1]
Devote yourselves to prayer, being watchful and thankful.[2]

I asked a group of forty Christian men recently to describe their devotional lives. They were asked to respond to three questions:

1. How many days a week do you set aside time to connect with God in focused, intentional prayer?
2. When you pray what is the average amount of time you pray?
3. On a scale of 1-10 how fulfilling, enjoyable, life-giving are those times of prayer?

I made it safe to respond honestly by allowing their responses to be anonymous. Only 6 out of the 40 prayed 5 or more days a week. Only 4 of those prayed 30 minutes or more when they did pray. Most were hit or miss. These results were not that surprising: I've taken surveys like this on numerous occasions. What was encouraging to me was to see that most were at least a 5 on the scale of fulfillment when they did pray. What was discouraging to me was the fact that 30 out of the 40 men present had been Christians for at least 5 years!

Like the men I've surveyed, you may truly DESIRE to spend more time in prayer. Our spirits long to be with Jesus, but our bodies can't seem to drag our souls out of bed to meet with Him. It is possible to so DELIGHT in spending time with God that it becomes part of our life-style. The right motivations will be the key, but we will never bypass the need for DISCIPLINE. Most of us hate this part, but we know deep down there's no way around it.

DESIRE → **DISCIPLINE** → DELIGHT

We've got to make room in our schedule to seek God's presence or it won't happen. I love Mother Teresa's way of saying it: "If we really mean to pray and want to pray we must be ready to do it now. These are only the first steps toward prayer, but if we never make the first step with a determination, we will not reach the last one: the presence of God."

Some of you may just want to be "led by the Spirit" as to when you pray. You say: "Wouldn't it better just to pray throughout the day? You know, the *pray without ceasing* sort of deal."[3] A predetermined time may seem too rigid, too legalistic for you. But ironically, we become more spontaneous in prayer throughout the day when we have a consistent focused time at some point during the day. I like what John Dalrymple said, "The truth is that we only learn to pray all the time, everywhere after we've resolutely set about praying some of the time, somewhere."

It's not that complicated. You schedule it. You do it. And if you just can't seem to do it, get some help.

Schedule it.

Find out when in your day is the best time for you to connect with God. For most of us that time is when we first get out of bed. You may say: "I'm just not a morning person." If some other time works better for you, go for it. A friend of mine takes his lunch hour to seek the Lord. Another friend sets aside time after the kids are in bed. Here's my observation: If you don't schedule it, it won't happen. It is like seeing a friend and you say, "Let's have lunch some time," and it never happens. You could be saying that same intention for the next ten years. Until you pull out our palm pilots or day-planner and set a date, it won't happen.

How long should I pray?

My answer to that question is "enough." Pray enough. Pray as long as it takes to find freedom in your heart from all of the crud and junk in your life. Pray until you feel all of the burdens and stress you are carrying have been transferred to God.[4] Pray until you have broken through to a place of trust, until you sense victory and joy in your soul, until you have connected with God and heard what He wants for you that day. How long does that take? It takes me more than fifteen minutes. (I love what my friend Jimmy Siebert says: "Fifteen minutes a day with God is barely enough time to stay out of major sin, much less change the world.") Most days I'm just getting warmed up at thirty minutes. It's easy for me to spend an hour or more with God. Honestly, it's been years since I've timed how long I pray. It's so life-giving I don't even think, "Have I logged my hour today?"

What if we don't FEEL any kind of emotional breakthrough in our prayer time?

What about seasons of dryness—the *dark night of the soul* stuff? You know, the times God seems so distant and your prayers seem like their dribbling off your chin and falling to the floor. I've had those seasons. But when I actually lay out my heart before God, the clouds are dispelled, at least to some degree. There is an increased lightness of soul, some level of joy I experience that I didn't have when I began praying. After all, isn't it God's desire to *show us how high, wide, long and deep is his love for us*—that we might experience His personal love for us?[5]

Just do it.

I know many people who have tried to establish some sort of consistent devotional life and failed, not once or twice, but numerous times. There's so much guilt and frustration associated with daily prayer, they just don't want to try it again and feel shame of failure over and over again. The key to becoming *consistent* in prayer is to be *persistent* in prayer. Years ago I "committed" to pray every day. I failed to follow through after a couple of days, and then I beat myself up. That was until I realized that the key is to *keep starting over*. If I missed Monday, I would start over on Tuesday. If I missed Wednesday, I would start over on Thursday. Connecting with God just three or four days a week was better than not praying at all. I kept starting over. (I lost count, but I think it was more than a hundred times of starting over). Prayer eventually became a pattern, a habit, a life-style.

You say, "I m not a very disciplined person." I can relate. That's where we need the Spirit of God to work healthy motivations into our hearts. Our desperation, the conviction that prayer makes a difference, and most of all, the love of God overpowers the inertia of our lack of discipline. When we began to delight in the presence of God, we make time for prayer. We need about as much "discipline" as a kid who is told he must eat his M & M's or an ice cream cone. "No *problemo*, Mom!"

Get help if you need it.

Most of us need accountability until it becomes our life-style—until we reach the stage in which prayer becomes our DELIGHT. I have some friends who frequently ask each other about their devotional lives. They realize that the best way they can love each other is spurring each other on toward the goals God has for their lives. There is such strength in following through with spiritual disciplines with the help of our Christian community. We need loving accountability. I know some guys that call each other at

5:30 each morning to make sure they are out of bed and going for it in prayer. A friend of mine will challenge the men he works with to pray. When they fail or make lame excuses, he actually meets with them and teaches them how to pray, day after day, until they get it.

You may ask: "Does it ever get easy to pray daily?" Even after years of this kind of life-style I must still exercise my will to pray. Rarely do I feel enthusiastic about prayer when I first crawl out of bed. I like how Graham Cooke says his daughter describes daily prayer: "Sometimes I can take the elevator to the penthouse suite to meet with God. More often, I must take the stairs."

Now for some profound advice for those of you having a difficult time waking up early enough to pray: *Go to bed earlier!* It's really a simple choice. You can watch Jay Leno, or you can turn off the TV and go to bed. You then will feel fresh enough to pray early tomorrow morning. It's not about the discipline you need to actually set your alarm (and not hit the snooze button). It's the discipline you need to go to bed at a decent hour.

Giving focus and energy to our time with God is so worth it because it will be life to us. We do what we perceive as being important for our lives. I have a friend who never exercised until he found out he had a heart condition. He now walks every day. He gets his walk in wherever he is, even on vacation. I once saw him walking late at night. He walks "religiously" as if his life depended on it. It does!

The truth is that you have a heart condition, whether you know it or not. Let's make the time to pray as if our life depended on it. Because it does!

Prayer Lab

1. What's the ideal time in your day for you to set aside time to pray?

2. Schedule a specific time to pray tomorrow if it's not already a routine in your life.

Chapter 4

Discover Your Prayer Style

Our preferences in connecting with God will vary as much as our personality types and quirks. Finding the best way and place for you to pray will help you pray more richly and consistently.

Find a place to pray alone.

Some actually find it much easier to pray with others than by themselves. My daughter Misi is now serving in Indonesia on the island of Papua, where she gets a very close-up look at how Indonesians approach their "quiet times." While living in a dorm which hosted her and a summer missions team, she thought it was amusing to see the differences between the Americans and Indonesians early in the mornings. The Americans would all be sitting by themselves in quiet places of solitude, listening to worship music on their headphones, Bibles and journals open, praying in silence. The more boisterous Papuans would be congregated in groups of three or four, banging out worship songs on guitars, loudly singing and calling out prayers together.

Is this just a cultural thing? Does our preference in prayer have to do with whether we are an extrovert (getting our batteries charged with others) or an introvert (getting charged up more by being alone)? It's true: there's a dynamic synergy in joining with others in prayer. We desperately need to pray in the context of our Christian community—friends, family, roommates, etc. The Holy Spirit is present in a unique way in corporate prayer. I encourage men to pray with their wives and fathers to pray with their children. But the Word also makes a strong case for solitude in your personal daily time with God.

But when you pray, close the door and pray to your Father, who is unseen. Then your Father, who sees what is done in secret will reward you...[1] Jesus often withdrew to lonely places and prayed.[2] We need to find a place where we can meet God alone. No radio. No TV. No children. No roommates. No answered phone calls. Henri Nouwen said, "Without solitude it is virtually impossible to live a spiritual life."

I know some people who have a literal *prayer closet* in their homes. It's so important to designate a place in or around our homes where we can routinely meet with God. Throughout our married life, Janine and I have chosen places to live where we are certain to have a place to pray. Balconies are ideal. A deck in the back yard will do. We once purchased a home that backed up to a huge ranch. I often took walks in the woods behind that house to commune with God. But my favorite place to pray was pacing back and forth on the back patio. A developer purchased the land directly behind us and began to build a subdivision. I was bummed. I felt my privacy was invaded when our new neighbor Harry had his deck built six feet from our back fence. When he sat on his deck he looked directly into our back yard. At first I was a bit inhibited in my prayer routine, but I got over it. I figured Harry might benefit from overhearing the things I was telling God. I didn't need to tell Harry about the joy of a living, dynamic relationship with God. He witnessed it in action.

Thomas Merton wrote: "My chief joy is to escape to the attic of the garden house and the little broken window that looks over the valley. There in the silence I love the green grass. The tortured gestures of the apple trees have become part of my prayer...So much do I love this solitude that when I walk out along the road to the old barns that stand alone, far from the new buildings, delight begins to overpower me from head to foot and peace smiles even in the marrow of my bones."

We can learn to pray anywhere. I've had wonderful times of prayer in my car, in airplanes, on trains, and buses. I recently returned from a mission trip where I slept in 27 different rooms (some of them quite primitive) over the course of 60 days. The presence of God was very real to me in all of those places. Several times when I felt boxed in a tiny bedroom with less than ideal conditions, I remembered the testimonies of Christians who have spent time in prison for the sake of gospel. Many speak of how sweet the presence of the Holy Spirit was, even in their small prison cell. We can really pray in any old place, provided we make it as distraction-free as possible.

For the purposes of your daily prayer routine you need a designated place. I know of a pastor who struggled with his personal prayer times. He said: "Whenever I show up at my designated place of prayer and I don't sense God's presence and I don't have a breakthrough in prayer, I still know that God knows I am there to meet Him."

Try praying out loud

One reason you need to be alone is so you can pray out loud. I know this may sound strange to you, but consider the prayers we find in the Bible. How many of them are *think-prayers*? Prayer is articulated, voiced, spoken. Meditation is silent. Daniel got in trouble because he was praying.[3] Had he been "praying" like most North American evangelicals he would have stayed out of the lion's den. Early followers of Jesus expressed their prayers out loud: *And when they heard this they raised their voices together in prayer to God.*[4] Even the written prayers in the Bible are recorded prayers that were once prayed aloud. They come down to us through inspiration of the Holy Spirit to be prayed—vocalized, read out loud, recited or quoted.

Most Christians from non-western nations voice their prayers. We once lived on a campus of a Bible school in Indonesia. Every morning at 5 a.m. we were awakened by a chorus of prayer coming out of the dorms, the chapel, and every class room. It was loud and intense. The students were going for it. I loved it! It made me eager to get up and pray. I'm told that they had made a rule before we moved there—no praying out loud until 5 a.m.! Apparently, the students had a habit of waking up and praying even earlier than five o'clock!

Many men I know have a hard time focusing their thoughts until they've learned to pray out loud. When we *think-pray* our minds tend to wander—drifting toward lunch, the tasks of the day, our favorite sports team, or sex. (I'm told women tend to think more about other things.) Praying out loud refocuses us and has revolutionized the prayer lives of many people I know.

What about praying in your car during commuter traffic? Won't people think you are crazy—talking to yourself and all? I've discovered a way to keep from looking weird. It's the hands free speaker set for your cell phone. Put on your head set, then you can drive down the road and just pray out loud all that you want. No one will think anything. If you are really brave, you can try this in the grocery store!

A disclaimer: obviously you can pray without speaking out your prayer. You do it all the time, before an important business meeting, when you are watching your kid performing in the school play, or even tidying up the house for company. We will always find occasions when *think-prayers* are more appropriate. But my point is this: praying out loud is the norm, especially if you want an extended, focused conversation with the Lord.

Find your best praying posture.

Some people like to kneel when they pray. Others like to stand, sit or lie prostrate (I tend to fall asleep in this position). My preference is to pace. It helps me focus. It's a bit annoying to my wife who prefers to sit and pray. But after years of my pacing she's handling it better. Out of courtesy I usually leave the room where we normally pray and prayer-pace somewhere else so as not to distract her.

Obviously, I can't pace while I journal or read the Word, but during the prayer part I get up and walk around. The key is to find your own prayer style. You can find a biblical example for almost any posture of prayer. Why not try different ones and see which ones works best for you?

Prayer Lab

1. Where's the best place in or nearby where you live where you can meet with God? Meet Him there next time you pray.

2. If praying out loud is new to you, try it out. Start with reading a psalm out loud, then express to God some of the things on your heart.

3. Try a new prayer posture. See how it feels.

Chapter 5

Keeping a Prayer Journal

In 1977 Janine and I were driving through the Arizona desert on the way to Southern California where I was to attend Fuller Seminary. We were excited to be launching out on our first adventure as a couple and confident that we were doing what God had called us to do; but we were a little anxious about the challenges that awaited us. As we shared our dreams and fears about moving to L.A., we had an idea. We decided to write out our prayers for this new season of life. We got very specific about housing, jobs, child care for our infant daughter, and a church home. One of our prayers was that God would provide a two-bedroom apartment for $200 a month or less within walking distance of the campus (Sort of dates us, doesn't it?). In less than a month, by God's great grace, four of these five prayers were answered! Our apartment on Los Robles turned out to be a great place for community close to campus at $195/month. The fifth request—a church home—came within the next month! There was no magic in our writing out these prayers, but we learned the faith-building power of recording our prayers. This became the very first entry in my first prayer journal.

There are times when I can best communicate with God through writing. There's a saying: "Thoughts untangle and make sense when they move through lips or fingertips." Sometimes my prayers flow easier through pen and ink. I don't feel pressure to write down every single prayer that I pray, but I jot down what I am generally feeling and praying. I write out expressions of my heart that are hard to vocalize, and then I read them out loud to the Lord. I confess my sins (I use Indonesian when I'm confessing the real incriminating stuff). I'm brutally honest about my struggles. I tell God how I feel, even the negative emotions. I write out the longings of my heart, my praises to Him, things for which I'm grateful, my petitions, and my fears. Someone reading my journal entries would think I'm writing God a letter—often it sounds like a love letter. I write down what I sense God is saying to me today.

There are at least five benefits I've discovered in keeping a prayer journal:

1. I have a record of some of my prayers, those answered and those yet to be answered. My faith is greatly built as I read over the journals I've kept for more than twenty-eight years.
2. I can track what God is teaching me through His Word and my life experiences. I listen better with my journal and pen in hand (I'll explain later the power of praying scriptures. I can't imagine praying in this way without using a prayer journal).
3. I can often better express the inner places of my heart to the Lord after I have articulated them on paper.
4. I can better communicate with Janine and my closest friends the essence of my interaction with God. At the end of our personal prayer times Janine and I often share what we've recorded in our journals in order to more effectively and intimately pray for each other.

My prayer journal reminds me to pray my "crafted" prayers that I repeat often to God. (More on this later.)

How often do I make an entry in my journal? For the first ten years of keeping a prayer journal, it seems I recorded some of the things I was praying two or three times a week. I now use it more often, usually around six days a week. But I'm not bound by it. It's a tool. I don't write for the sake of filling up journals or checking off a box. I use it to express my heart to God.

If you'd like, you can use different symbols in your journal to designate different ways of communicating your heart to God. For example I use [ ] to denote prayers. The symbol { } reflects thoughts, ideas, prophetic impressions that God seems to be want to communicate to me. A "*" can symbolize things for which I am grateful. I usually number my requests, and I also try to quote and reference passages from the Bible.

Finally, I don't recommend using a dated journal. It might be too depressing to see all of those blank pages! I give myself plenty of grace in this.

Here's an example of a typical entry:

June 13, 2004 - Bali, Indonesia

This so describes what You've done for me, Father: He reached down from heaven; He drew me out from the deep waters. He delivered me from my powerful enemies...despair, loneliness, discouragement, defeat, heaviness of heart. Way to go, God! Indeed, they were too strong for me...They attacked me at the moment I was weakest. BUT THE LORD UPHELD ME. He lead me to a place of safety (Psalm 18:16-19 NLT). You've led me here by Your Spirit. Each place I've been on this journey YOU rescued me because You delighted in me. It's hard to wrap my heart around that, but I choose to believe it. You are wooing me to Yourself - that place of safety. Old enemies like sexual fantasies have showed up here but they are defeated.

* Thank you for the strength and inner joy I feel

at this stage of my journey. I so love FEELING Your presence. I know You were there last week when I didn't feel You. Thanks for the grace to fast. I'm confident that You are listening to the cry of my heart today.

* Thanks for the chance to meet Bryan and Debbie. I would love to share more about You with them.

* Thanks also for the beach, access to the internet, and great fruit juice.

* Thanks for Rabi Maharaja's awesome testimony - I have new compassion for the Hindus of this island.

(From 2 Corinthians 4 NLT)
What a vivid description what I'm ASKING FOR, on this trip, in Surabaya, in Austin...
and wherever we send HFN teams; And as God's grace brings more and more people to Christ...More disciples resulting in...great thanksgiving and God will receive more and more glory (verse 15). Please Lord, more worship, more worshipers, more worshiping communities.
* Let my spirit be renewed today, even though my 49 year old body feels like it's wasting away.
* May I joyfully endure the loneliness, the hunger pains, the "work" of prayer and planning.

Hopefully you get the picture (I'll resist the temptation to explain my thoughts that day). My prayer journal entries are rarely more than a page or two. They are more like sketchy outlines of what I am praying. After I've jotted down these thoughts, I then read them out loud, expounding on the points that inspire me.

This discipline has so enhanced my prayer life and relationship with God that I urge you to at least give it a try! It will revolutionize your journey with Him.

Prayer Lab

1. Write a letter to God. Express the things for which you are grateful. Write out some of the deepest longings of your heart.

2. After you're finished, read it out loud, elaborating on any of the points in your personal prayers to God.

Chapter 6

All Kinds of Prayers

*And pray in the Spirit on all occasions with **all kinds of prayers** and requests.*[1]

I'm going to admit something not usually confessed publicly— prayer can be boring. People have a difficult time maintaining a consistent, meaningful devotional life because they run out of things to say. I remember when I was new at all this. I would pray everything I could think to pray, then glance at my watch and see that I had prayed for only ten minutes! Going through this spiritual exercise daily was about as much fun as clipping my fingernails.

My prayers then were one dimensional—namely me communicating my request to God. "Lord, Bless Aunt Mabel." "Please help me to do well on my test." "Help the Dallas Cowboys win this week." You get the picture. And then I would feel guilty that I wasn't praying longer, but the truth was ten minutes felt too long already.

The good news is that our relationship with God can be far more multidimensional—more diverse in our communication patterns. It's just like a good marriage. Married couples who enjoy healthy intimacy connect on many levels. Obviously, physical intimacy is important. But there are other types of intimacy that a couple can enjoy that enhance the relationship. Having fun together is important. Some couples find a hobby they share. There is also intimacy that comes through creating something together, like starting a business, building a house, or landscaping the yard together. Sharing a love for art, music, or travel enriches a relationship. Janine and I really enjoy so many different kinds of intimacy together and it has greatly enhanced our relationship. What if the only thing we did together every day is communicate about the day's "to-do" list? How lifeless and boring our relationship would be. That's how your prayer life might feel right now.

The broader the communication, the greater level of intimacy a couple enjoys. Isn't the same true in our relationships with God? When I begin to relate to Him as more than just the big vending machine in the sky, my heart is caught up and captured by knowing Him.

We can learn to pray prayers of thanksgiving, prayers of adoration, prayers of repentance and confession, prayers of submission and surrender. Sometimes prayer can be like doing battle. I call these *kingdom warfare prayers*. "Lord, let the enemies of depression be scattered over my friend Mark. Rise up on his behalf, Father."

We can become skilled in making bold, specific requests for the needs of others. "Lord, I ask today that You would come through for John in the devastating aftermath of him losing his job. Please provide financially for him today so that he could know You are his provider. Give him peace that You will provide for his family. I pray for good job contacts this very week, Lord."

We can pray the prayers of the Bible. "Father in heaven, I believe in Your character today. Every good and perfect gift comes down from You, Father of Lights. You don't turn like shifting shadows. I turn from self-sufficiency and into Your loving arms." Mike Bickle says that praying scriptures greatly increases your "prayer vocabulary" and stretches you into new territory of God's kingdom and His heart.

We can turn what we read in the Word into prayer. Prayers like these are always fresh. This morning in a men's discipleship class I put up a passage from 1 Thessalonians on an overhead and different guys took turns praying different verses out loud. After that I took the same overhead to a staff meeting, where we began our time by praying different themes from the same passage, taking each sentence into new directions. Both times people selected the same verses and prayed totally different prayers. It was great fuel for our intercession. The Word of God through prayer is living, active and exciting!

If we prayed with this kind of variety, our prayers would never be boring. Even prayers we repeat can be fresh and dynamic. We're not just reciting lines from a play, but we are playing a part in a great drama when we connect with God's heart creatively. It's as unique and imitate as your best relationships—even better. It can be as sweet as a kid sitting in his dad's lap. There we receive His affirmation, His correction, or His intimate counsel.

Prayer patterns

Most people who pray consistently have a routine or pattern that they follow. In my spiritual journey these patterns or outlines of prayer were helpful in establishing a more consistent routine in my life of connecting with the Lord. I am indebted to these well-used models of prayer. You may find them helpful as well. Later in the book we'll get into more diverse forms of prayer, but try these first for starters:

A Prayer List

Make the following topics the focus of your prayers on a specific day of each week:

Monday - Family

Tuesday - Government Leaders

Wednesday - Non-Christian friends and family members

Thursday - Your Christian community and friends

Friday - Missionaries and unreached peoples

Saturday - Personal needs

Sunday - Your church and pastors

ACTS

Pray the following outline daily:

- Adoration - Begin with prayers of praise and adoration, exulting the greatness of God.
- Confession - Search you heart and confess any known sins.
- Thanksgiving - Let gratefulness overflow for specific ways God has blessed you.
- Supplication - Bring requests, petitions, and your needs before God.

The Lord's Prayer Outline

I prayed according to this outline most days of the week for nearly a decade of my life:

Matthew 6:9-13

Our Father in heaven, hallowed be your name...
- Focus on the names and character attributes of God
- Pray prayers of adoration and affection

Your kingdom come, Your will be done on earth as it is in heaven...
Invite God's kingly reign (His will) into:
- Your life, your family, your day, and your work
- Your church and Christian community
- Your city
- The nation and other nations of the world (political leaders, missions, church planting movements, etc.)
- Your friends and acquaintances who are lost

Give us today our daily bread...
- Bring your needs and requests to God

Forgive us our debts, as we also have forgiven our debtors...
- Confess areas of sin and repentance
- Pray for relationships that may be strained or in conflict
- Check your heart attitudes toward everyone, especially those people with whom you are frustrated

And lead us not into temptation, but deliver us from the evil one...
- Pray for any area in which you are facing temptation
- Clothe yourself in the armor of God (Ephesians 6)

For Yours is the kingdom, and the power and the glory forever
Close with adoration and thanksgiving

If you are struggling with trying to get a consistent, meaningful time with God, I urge you to try these basic prayer patterns this week. Let these training wheels get you started into a new, exciting journey with God.

In the proceeding chapters we will walk through **all kinds of prayers** you can learn to incorporate into your times with the Lord. I will do my best to explain them and give examples. But unless you try them, this book will have little impact in your growth into a dynamic relationship with the living God. Follow through on the prayer labs at the end of each chapter, and your spiritual life will be lifted into new dimensions of knowing and loving God. In Chapter 18, I will give you another example of an outline you can follow that will make prayer even more dynamic and life-giving for you.

Prayer Lab

Choose one of the prayer patterns listed in this chapter and try it out for a day or two. Reflect on how it may have helped your prayer time.

Chapter 7

Prayers of Gratitude and Thanksgiving

*No matter what happens, always be **thankful**, for this is God's will for you who belong to Jesus Christ* (1 Thessalonians 5:18 NLT).

*...Continue to live in Him, rooted and built up in Him, strengthened in the faith as you were taught, and overflowing with **thankfulness*** (Colossians 2:7).

*...But in everything, by prayer and petition, with **thanksgiving**, present your request to God* (Philippians 4:6).

Having a heart overflowing with thankfulness doesn't come naturally. Maybe you're different, but rarely do I roll out of bed on a groggy morning with a grateful heart. It feels much easier to complain and be critical. I must choose to be thankful. For most of us, our default mode is to murmur. We have to work at an attitude of gratitude. We "will to" be grateful, and then usually our emotions follow.

Just this morning I was feeling kind of crabby as I made my morning cup of coffee. There was too much to do today and not enough time to do it all and some unresolved issues from yesterday that needing addressing today. I felt all those gray thoughts fogging my mind right from the get-go. Instead of dwelling on them, I decided the first place I needed to go was thankfulness. Before long the cloud disappeared and my spirit was overflowing with gratitude with all the ways God has met me.

Here's where a prayer journal is so helpful. Start your "letter to God" with a list of the things for which you are truly grateful. You may at first say: "Nothing comes to mind." Work at it, and gratitude will begin to flow. You just need to "prime the pump." Start listing them:

+ Simple, seemingly mundane "blessings" of the last 24 hours
+ Specific answers to prayer
+ People God has brought into your life whom you truly appreciate
+ What He is teaching through your life experiences
+ Broad, eternal truths of what God has done for us in Christ
+ Promises, hopes, and encouraging insights from what you are reading in the Bible
+ Things you've asked God for that you are confident He is doing: present your request with thanksgiving!

Here's an example of my journal entry on June 29:

Father, I do so appreciate:

* A great night's sleep
* Time with Misi and Julie
* A good international phone connection with Janine and Heather. I am so excited about seeing Janine in 3 days.
* A good swim-2 days in a row!
* Jeff-I loved getting some time with him yesterday. Thank you for his friendship. I was so encouraged last night when he pointed out my trip to Sumbawa has been such an inspiration to him and others.

*The fun of shopping! (Can you believe I'm saying this?)

*For speaking to me through *Cry the Beloved Country*. I'm loving it.

After I made this list, I read it out loud to God. Notice, I wasn't theologically profound or prolific in the gratitude I expressed. But it was sincere and from my heart.

You can also turn almost any chapter in the Bible into a prayer of thanksgiving (not withstanding some parts of Leviticus that could be rather challenging!) I prayed the first chapter of Ephesians yesterday, and I was so captivated by the richness of God's grace I prayed it again this morning. Here's an example of part of my "thankful list" that flowed out of Ephesians 1:

* I praise You for every spiritual blessing I have in Christ Jesus
* Thank you for the incredible knowledge that You have initiated relationship with me – You chose me in Christ before the creation of the world
* Your plan was to make me holy and blameless
* I am experiencing Your kindness
* I am adopted into Your family
* I am FREE through the blood of Christ.

That is barely a third of the way through my list, but I think you get the picture.

Nothing ushers us into the presence of God like gratitude. *Enter His gates with thanksgiving and His courts with praise.*[1] I met with a group of men from our church for early morning prayer last week. A quick read on the other guys in the room gave me the strong impression they were asking the same question that had come to my mind: "Now why did I crawl out of bed at 5:00 AM to get here?" Obviously, I wasn't the only one there who had felt it had been a short night. There seemed to be zero passion to jump into an intense time of intercession. So I suggested we jot down a list of things for which we are grateful—specific ways in which God was demonstrating His love in our lives. I gave the guys about 10 minutes. They took 15. We then stood up, held up our lists and began to speak out loud the things we had just written on our scraps of paper. The atmosphere in the room was dramatically transformed. Some of us soon began shouting. Others were sobbing. God showed up. I had an overwhelming sense of the Lord's pleasure in our willful choice to express our gratitude. *Since we are receiving a Kingdom that cannot be destroyed, let us be thankful and please God....*[2]

I practice this discipline of thankfulness daily. I become truly grateful as I *do* gratitude. More importantly, God is so worthy of my sincere gratitude. I often feel like I could never repay God's gracious gifts to me. But like the leper, I at least want to come back to Him and tell Him how much I appreciate His profound work in my life.[3]

Prayer Lab

1. Make a thankful list.

2. Now, pray your list—read it out loud to the Lord.

Chapter 8

Prayers of Adoration and Praise

Try this next time you pray. Better yet, next time you are asked to lead a prayer time, suggest this to the group: "Let's not ask God for anything for the first ten minutes. Instead, let's pray prayers expressing our love and adoration to God. Let's focus on His attributes, His worthiness." Let me predict what will happen. You or someone in your prayer group will start to jump into prayers of petition before the ten minutes are up. Cultivating this kind of prayer in my prayer times was challenging for me because:

1. I ran out of things to say.
2. At times, it felt insincere.
3. I equated prayer with asking for things.
4. I was more *me-centered* than *God-centered* (hard to admit but true). Prayer was more about me and my needs!

Prayers of adoration and praise are prayers in which we exalt the greatness of God. We focus on His person and His character and attributes and express our affection to Him. Biblical examples of these kinds of prayers are numerous. In fact, it's hard to find prayers in the Word that don't include prayers of adoration and praise. Most begin with profound acknowledgment of the Person of God.

O Lord, God of our fathers, are you not the God who is in heaven? You rule over all the kingdoms of the nations. Power and might are in your hand, and no one can withstand You. O our God, did You not drive out the inhabitants of this land before Your people Israel and gave it to the descendants of Abraham your friend? [1] King Jehoshaphat prayed this way when he faced the overwhelming forces of Ammon and Moab. Our tendency would be to jump right to the request: "Help us out here, God. These Ammonites and Moabites are too much for us." But notice he began his prayer with a recognition of the person of God. The prayer outline Jesus gave us begins with *Father who is in heaven, may your name be honored....* [2]

Not only is God is so worthy of these kinds of prayers, but I've noticed that something happens in us when we pray this way. We become who we were meant to be when we bring glory to God. We align our frantic souls under His lordship. We get perspective. Our faith level rises. We begin to see God for who He really is.

God is everything we need Him to be. He is redeemer, healer, shepherd, provider, comfort, protector, friend—He is more awesome than we can ever conceive. When we acknowledge these aspects of His character and repeat them back to Him they somehow become more real to us. The reality of God moves from our heads to our hearts. We realize He is *our* redeemer, *our* healer, *our* shepherd, etc. They are real whether we acknowledge or not, but we can awaken ourselves to that reality by verbally reciting aspects of God's character back to Him.

We can praise God for the sun shining even on a rainy day when we can't see the shining sun through the rain clouds. Our hearts will begin to shine more when we do that for which we were created—glorify God for who He is.

Let me suggest a couple of ways to sustain and engage your heart in praise and adoration:

Use worship music

I have friends who begin their time with God with a guitar in hand. If you are not musically inclined, put on your favorite worship CD. I have often used a hymnal in my prayer times. I sing, recite, and pray one or two of my favorite hymns. Whatever floats your worship boat, do it!

List of the names for God and Jesus found in the Word

Pray your list: "God, You are my Jehovah-jireh (provider)." "I praise You for being my Shepherd." As I read through the Gospel of John, I was caught up in all the names of Jesus—the light of the world, the bread of life, the way, the truth, the life, the vine. It sparked fresh devotion in my heart as I read those back to God.

Find fresh vocabulary to describe God's character

Several years ago my friend Jamey Miller inspired me with this idea. Using a thesaurus and a dictionary he came up with a list of words in an attempt to describe the attributes of God. I tried it, too, compiling words from the dictionary in alphabetical order: awesome, approachable, authentic, aggressive, almighty, always, beautiful, bountiful, blessed, brilliant, caring, capable, champion, clear, colorful, communicative, deep, daring, delightful, dear, dynamic, enduring, edifying, eminent, enthroned, forgiving, faithful, factual, firm, gracious, gallant, gentle, and good natured. He is holy, healing. He is high. He is helpful. (I get excited just reading my list, which this is just a small fraction.) God is inviting, ideal, immense, joyful, jealous, and jovial. He is kind. He is kingly. He is kaleidoscopic (K's are challenging). He is keeper, and king. He is loving. He is longsuffering. He is large. He is lord. You get the idea. Now get out your dictionary and give it a try!

Communicate your love and affection

I find a growing freedom in simply verbally expressing my love to God. I often tell Him how much I love Him. "I love You more than…my wife…my children…my work…my life…." This may sound a bit cheesy, especially to guys, but it really *is* what we are created to do—to love God! Open your mouth in expressions of adoration, and I promise you your heart will follow.

There have been many days when I've become so "caught up" in prayers of thanksgiving, praise, and adoration I ran out of time to pray anything else. Do you think this might be okay with God?

In the 1700's, God touched the life of a wealthy young man, Nicholas Ludwig von Zinzendorf. He was part of German nobility, living a life of ease and luxury when God radically changed his life one day as he visited a museum. He saw a painting of Jesus being crucified and he heard an inner voice say, "I have done all this for you. What will you do for me?" Zinzendorf gave his life fully to God, and when he got older he opened his estate in the Saxony mountains to a group of Moravians who were fleeing persecution from their own country. He, along with members of this displaced and bickering community, were visited mightily by the Spirit on August 13, 1727. The revival that started that evening launched a continual prayer meeting that lasted for the next 100 years! Under Count Zinzendorfs leadership, their little community in the next two decades sent out more missionaries than all Protestants and Anglicans have sent out in the previous two centuries. We know them today as the Moravians. Their movement, within the next 150 years, sent out a total of 2,158 members as missionaries to countries all over the world![3]

What was the secret of this one man whom God used so mightily to impact so many nations, and whose life still impacts people today? The guy just oozed love for Jesus. It is said that when he walked by, people heard him constantly mutter under his breath things like, "Oh, Fairest Lord Jesus," or other expressions of praise. He was caught up in loving God so much that he was thought to be a little odd. He wrote hundreds and hundreds of hymns in his lifetime, so overflowing with praise and adoration to the Lord. God used Him, yes. But Count Zinzendorf was caught up more in the awesome wonder and privilege of knowing God.

We've all just scratched the surface of knowing God. It's going to take an entire eternity to realize how amazingly great God is. But we can dig a little deeper today.

Prayer Lab

1. In your next prayer time, designate the first 15 minutes for expressing to God how good He is and how much you love Him. Resist the temptation to bring petitions to God—just enjoy His attributes.

2. If you run out of things to say, sing or recite some of your favorite worship songs.

3. Use the names and character traits of God and Jesus to adore Him.

4. Use a dictionary to make a short list of ways God the Father has made Himself known to you.

Chapter 9

Prayers of Confession and Repentance

I'll never forget the first time I was able to really open up and be honest about my struggle with sin with some of my friends. We were a group of college freshmen guys who were trying to follow Jesus. It was late at night in a dorm room and one of the guys courageously confessed slipping back into smoking marijuana. His example inspired the rest of us. One after another we came clean. We shared about our lust, our lies, our addictions, and our hypocrisy. There were tears of shame, and then...tears of joy at sensing God's forgiveness. We prayed for each other. We claimed the promises of God's mercy. We felt close, like a "band of brothers." We celebrated the freedom of a clean conscience before God and each other.[1] I learned something extremely important that night: confession and repentance is the only way to live in freedom from the power of sin.

The more we press into the presence of God through worship, adoration, and thanksgiving, the more our hearts become sensitized to our own sin. Like the prophet Isaiah, when we see the Lord *high and lifted up* and get a fresh glimpse of His holiness we say: *I am a sinful man....*[2] We become painfully aware of our thoughts, attitudes, and actions that have displeased the Lord. We clearly see the gap.

With God, there's no posing, no excuses, no need to impress Him with our piety. He sees us as we really are and He *desires honesty from the heart.*[3] There's such freedom to bare our souls before Him. One of the works of the Holy Spirit is to convict us of our sin and He's extremely competent at His job.[4] You and I can pray: *Search me, O God, and know my heart; test my heart; test me and know my thoughts. Point out anything that offends you....*[5] The Holy Spirit is all over that kind of prayer.

When God convicts us we can choose to humble ourselves and confess our sins. The Greek word for confession, *homologeo,* can be broken down into *homo* which means "same" and *logeo* which means "to speak." So to confess, *homolego*, means literally "to say the same thing." Confession is simply agreeing with the Holy Spirit. When He says, "Your attitude toward _____ is wrong," or "You haven't paid that money back yet..." or "Those words that you said to your wife hurt her," we can just agree. No need to argue or debate or make excuses. Just agree. "You are right, I spoke harshly to my wife." "I am so sorry that I misjudged his motives without really hearing him out." "I shouldn't have done that. Please forgive me and cleanse my heart." I've often made Psalm 51 my personal prayer. *Have mercy on me, O God according to Your unfailing love; according to Your great compassion blot out my transgressions. Wash away all my iniquity and cleanse me from my sin.*[6]

It's important to receive God's forgiveness when we've blown it. I've prayed this promise hundreds of times: *If you confess your sins, He is faithful and just and will forgive us our sins, and cleanse you from all unrighteousness.*[7] "Lord, as I have confessed my sin before You, I now receive Your full pardon for my sin—all of my unrighteousness."

Repentance goes beyond admitting or acknowledging our wrong. To repent, *metanoeo,* means "to change directions" or "to change your mind." It requires that we *turn from* our previous direction or old way of living and *turn toward* God. This often requires an action that we need to live out. If I've sinned against someone, I need to go to them and ask forgiveness. Repentance might mean a difficult conversation or restitution. It means change.

Sometimes men confess to me their struggle with the sin of internet pornography. When I see them again later, I always ask, "How's it going?" because I know they have undoubtedly faced the temptation to log on again. God's purpose for them is that they walk in freedom. A friend confessed this sin to me previously, and then got some direct follow-up questions from me later that week. He said, "Thanks Ron, for not just mummy-cuddling me on this and letting me know of God's forgiveness, but also for asking me pointed questions and giving me a kick in the tail." He desired not only forgiveness, but repentance.

When we cultivate a life-style of intimacy with God we keep short accounts. Sin doesn't have a chance to gain a foothold in our hearts and keep us feeling bound, defeated, and condemned. We are daily laying out our souls before God and praying through our failures as they occur. Christian counselor Richard Dobbins has helped numerous church leaders in the aftermath of a moral failure. He has made a profound observation: none of these leaders were experiencing a daily time of focused, life-giving prayer when they "fell" into the trap of sexual immorality.

How does one distinguish between the conviction of the Holy Spirit and the condemning lies of our accuser—Satan? God always points out our sin—the specific behavior or attitude that is wrong. Satan blasts our person, our character. The Spirit reveals our sin in order to restore the joy of our intimacy with the Father. The enemy's voice leaves us feeling worthless and hopeless. Sincere confession and turning toward God brings *freedom*. God is intent on drawing us back to His heart. Louis Cassels said, "In confession...we open our lives to healing, reconciling, restoring, uplifting grace of Him who loves us in spite of what we are."

Here's a prayer I journaled a while back:

What regret I feel. I rented a loser video and foolishly didn't turn it off when I discovered how violent and wicked it was. I have such a sense of displeasing You, God. Lord, with all of my heart I recognize my own sin in exposing my eyes and thoughts to such trash. I made the choice based on my own lust for pleasure, and I am very ashamed. Please forgive me. Please wash me. Please renew my mind and my spirit today. I love You.

Should you confess and repent daily?

I seem to experience "seasons" of brokenness and repentance. For a period of time it seems like I'm repenting every day—throughout the day! Why? Because I am so aware of my offenses and how much I need His mercy and grace to cover my sin. However sometimes I don't sense any specific ways that I've grieved the Holy Spirit. I may need to settle my heart into a posture of listening prayer, just to make sure I'm being sensitive to His voice. I don't feel the need to confess and repent every day if my heart is pure before the Lord. He knows how often I truly need to repent because of my attitudes, words, or actions which have dishonored Him. The important thing is for our hearts to stay tender and open to Him so that we hear His whispers loud and clear.

From Duty To Delight

Prayer Lab

1. In your next prayer time, take a few minutes and invite the Holy Spirit to show you thoughts, attitudes, or actions that have displeased the Lord.

2. Write them out specifically in your prayer journal.

3. Personalize Psalm 51 by reading it out loud as your prayer of confession. Then read 1 John 1:8-9. Pray it as a promise for yourself.

4. Write out any specific ways you need to repent. What are the next action steps?

Chapter 10

Prayers of Submission and Surrender

The World has yet to see what God can do with, for, and through any man who is fully consecrated to Him. —D.L. Moody

A young teenager named Henry Parsons Crowell heard Moody say this while listening to him speak in a country church outside Chicago in 1873. He immediately slipped out of the back of the church and, on the dirt road that ran in front of the church, surrendered his life to Christ. As an adult he became known as the inventor of oatmeal and the founder and president of Quaker Oats. Many people of Chicago knew him as a sterling example of a Christian businessman. He led many to faith in Christ. For more than 50 years he consistently gave away over 70% of his income to build churches, fund ministries, and feed the poor in the Chicago area. He lived a life of surrender to Jesus Christ.

Every true follower of Christ has prayed a prayer of submission or surrender to God's will. Submission is where our relationship with the Lord begins. This kind of prayer ushers us into a faith relationship with God, and then we begin to be transformed by the grace of God. But we can pray that type of prayer daily. It's like the clay putting itself back on the potter's wheel every day. We "come under" God's kingly rule when we pray this way. To live in the place of intimacy that we so desire, we need to keep this posture of submission. However, we, as living sacrifices, tend to crawl off the altar. That's why we are told: *Submit* (a continuous or repeated action) *yourself, then, to God.*[1]

Everything within our carnal, fleshly self fights submission. Our nation was founded on a Declaration of Independence. The pride of men fights submitting to a higher authority at every turn. Karl Marx, the founder of communism, once wrote, "The social principles of Christianity preach cowardice, self-contempt, abasement, submission, humility, in a word all the qualities of the canaille (the masses of ignorant people)." He disdained what our pride also despises—that submission is for the weak.

That's what is rising up in us as we seek to make our bodies slaves to Christ. It's easy to fool ourselves into thinking that we are submitted to God when we're really not. That's why these prayers are so crucial. That's why we shouldn't pray them lightly.

We're familiar with Jesus' prayer of submission in the garden: *Not my will, but yours be done.*[2] He told His disciples: *For I have come down from heaven to do the will of God who sent me, not to do what I want.*[3] If Jesus needed to submit to the will of the Father, how much more do we need to *offer* (our) *bodies as living sacrifices, holy and pleasing to God—this is* (our) *spiritual act of worship.*[4] Just think, Jesus could have done anything He wanted: He could have lived in a nice palace, ordered people around with His power, destroyed His enemies with one word, done whatever He wanted. But He chose submission. He sweat drops of blood over this issue. Wouldn't that mean that this should be a struggle for us, if we are really submitting our life to Him?

Remember the scene from Mel Gibson's *Passion of the Christ* where Jesus is in the courtyard of the Roman soldiers and is getting whipped? He placed his hands on the wooden post voluntarily and prayed, "Father, my heart is ready." His heart was always ready—and ours can be too if we honestly pray these prayers of submission and overcome our innate desire to control our own lives.

From Duty To Delight

A pastor friend of mine tells about the impact a missionary had on his life who lived by the AAA creed: "Anything, Anytime, Anywhere." Total submission. Are you a "Triple-A" Christian? Don't answer too soon. Bring your list to God and then try to answer that question honestly. Are you willing to do anything, go anywhere, anytime for Jesus?

A prayer of submission or surrender is not passive resignation. It's a willful act of "handing over" every part of our lives to God. It's a transfer of ownership to God what's really already His if we are born again—*your life is not your own, you are bought with a price.*[5] A prayer of submission or surrender is an acknowledgment of a transfer of ownership. It goes like this: "Father I choose to offer to You...

- ❑ My day (tasks, appointments, plans, schedule, etc.)
- ❑ My relationships
- ❑ My wealth, resources, and possessions
- ❑ My gifts and talents
- ❑ My needs, longings, dreams, and desires
- ❑ My work and career
- ❑ My rights
- ❑ My life
- ❑ Anything else that comes to mind…

Don't pray these kind of prayers flippantly! Several years ago I was pacing on my back porch praying this kind of prayer. I was going down a mental list of "our" assets (It was a short list.): "Father, our cars are yours, our furniture is yours, our house is yours…." I was arrested with a distinct impression that God was taking me up on my offer. The thought occurred to me that we were to offer our (God's) house to some friends. We were not to make a profit off of it. In fact, we were to offer it for the amount we still owed on the house. In other words, we were to give away our equity. But it was not a dreadful, ominous thought to me. It was one that filled me with great joy. Needless to say, I needed to have this word confirmed, especially by my wife. You can bet I asked the Lord repeatedly if I were hearing correctly during the next few months while I worked up the courage to tell Janine what I had heard. It took her several months to have a peace about this decision. But then one day, out of the blue, she shared how the Lord had spoken to her as well. Like for me, this prompting was accompanied by great joy. We then invited our kids in on this process. They had the same grace. Bottom line, we offered the house to our friends and they joyfully accepted our offer. The timing was perfect.

Sometimes a prayer of submission or *relinquishment* (as the prayer masters of old called it) involves a struggle—a death to our will. Jesus asked that He not have to be crucified, yet He submitted to the will of the Father. Sometimes, there's pain in the offering. I often pray: "Lord, teach me to lose my life for your sake today that I may gain it. Help me live as one dead to self and truly alive to you." It's a sacrifice. In the Bible something dies when a sacrifice is given.

But here's the paradox: There is no greater joy than in total surrender. The definition of freedom is a heart totally given over to Him! It's a trade off in which we win big time! We give God what we have (which, when you think about it, is not that impressive) and in exchange, we experience *life that is truly life*.[6] Mother Teresa said it well: "The prize with which God rewards our self-abandonment is Himself."

William Booth, the 19th century revivalist and founder of the Salvation Army, said, "The greatness of a man's power is the measure of his surrender." The more we surrender, the more of Christ's power can work through us. God worked through William Booth's life powerfully to work great change in England and the world-wide body of Christ.

All of this was because he prayed a prayer of submission after feeling God's heavy conviction about his half-submitted life. These kinds of prayers might cost a lot, but they will bring greater heart intimacy with the Father and He will change the world through us as we pray them.

Prayer Lab

1. Take time to pray prayers of submission and surrender. Make it simple like: "Father I joyfully offer to you _____." Fill in the blank with everything that the Holy Spirit brings to mind.

2. Ask: "Lord is there something, some area of my life that I've been claiming as my own?" If He shows you something, lay it on "the altar" in prayer.

Chapter 11

Prayers of Request and Bold Petition

"Lord, please send a helicopter." It's not the kind of prayer that I typically pray, but during the month of January 2005 we prayed it on several occasions.

Janine and I led a medical relief team from our church to the island of Sumatra on the heels of the devastating tsunamis that killed over 150,000 people in that region. On January 13, our team, along with 40 bins of medical supplies, waited on the tarmac of the airport of Banda Aceh. Relief workers from numerous organizations found themselves there, stuck in the quagmire of chaos and bureaucracy in the attempt to find transportation into the most critical areas along the west coast of North Sumatra. God graciously answered our prayers and sent us not one, but four helicopters to fly us and our supplies into a region where no relief agencies had been.

We set up a temporary clinic just outside of what had been a town of 16,000 named Tenom. The homes, business, schools—nearly every structure had been destroyed and half of the residents had died or were still missing. During a five day period we treated over 300 patients, most of them refugees of the tsunami disaster. Nearly everyone we encountered had experienced trauma beyond what any of us could relate to. Most had lost several family members. We felt privileged to be the hands of Jesus caring for them and praying for them during those days. It was an amazing experience and by the end of the week we began to make plans for our departure. We had plane tickets from Medan, but we had no assurance that the U.S. Navy Seahawk that had dropped us off six days before would actually show up us to transport us out. To complicate matters we had no means of communicating with the outside world. On the morning we had to begin our journey home we packed our backpacks and made our way to the landing zone four kilometers away. To our delight a crowd had gathered to see us off. But there was no helicopter. We taught the crowd some worship songs and shared the gospel with them. But after a couple of hours we began to get a bit antsy. Someone said: "We haven't even asked God to send a helicopter today have we?" We joined hands in front of our Indonesian Muslim friends and prayed: "Lord, please send a helicopter." Within minutes we heard the beautiful sound of chopper blades. Way to go, God!

Most of us think of petitions and requests when we think of prayer. I am making a case for the need for *all kinds of prayers,* but prayers of petition are an important part of our prayer vocabulary. Asking God for whatever we need (and sometimes what we want) is not selfish or unhealthy. We're told to pray this way: *And pray in the Spirit on all occasions with all kinds of prayers and requests.*[1] *Pray about everything, tell God what you need.*[2]

Asking with boldness

Jesus taught that not only are we to ask, we are to ask **boldly**. In Luke 11, He teaches an outline we can use to pray (the Lord's Prayer) then He tells us what our attitude should be when we pray. He then tells a story about a guy who had a guest and needed to feed him (a common Middle Eastern custom). The man is out of bread so he goes to his neighbor and wakes him up and asks for three loaves of bread. His request is answered, but not because of friendship with his neighbor. Jesus says: *because of the man's boldness he will get up and give him as much as he needs.*[3] The operative word is *boldness*. It's from a Greek word that is a challenge to translate because the word is used nowhere else in the New Testament. However, the opposite form of the word is used when Paul describes how godly women should act— with propriety, politely.[4] The *ana* prefix in the Luke 11 word (*anaidian*) makes it negative. It literally means impropriety or rudeness. We would use the word *gall*. This is how were to pray—*with gall* !

Praying with *gall* means...

- asking even when we don t deserve it *(he will not get up and give him the bread because he is his friend)*.
- asking very specifically (*three loaves of bread*).
- not being overly concerned about the will or desires of the one we are asking. (*It's midnight and the kids are asleep.*)

God's will phobia

In a scene from the movie "Bruce Almighty," Jim Carey's character gets in a car wreck and meets God in heaven. "God," played by Morgan Freeman, stands in front of Bruce and asks him to make a prayer. Bruce is new at this and finally stammers out haltingly, "Lord, let there be world peace."

He opens his eyes to see God's reaction, and God tells him, "That was a beautiful prayer...." Bruce feels relieved.

Then God adds, "If you're a Miss America contestant." What Bruce really wanted was to be given a second chance to be reunited with his girlfriend. God was waiting for him to ask for that, which Bruce finally did, and God praised him for praying it from his heart.

This scene pointed out an underlying belief system that many have. We tend to be reluctant to ask God for what we really want, fearing that we are out of line or thinking somehow our prayers are contrary to God's will. We think somehow that we are going to throw a monkey wrench into God's sovereignty and mess up the kingdom of heaven for all eternity. The guy who rudely awakened his friend and asked for three loaves of bread didn't seem to be thinking: "I wonder if this is my friend's *will*?" Notice, he doesn't even say: "If it's okay with you…" or "If you don't mind…." He just went for it.

Jesus prayed thousands of prayers while on earth. To our knowledge only once did He add at the end *if it be your will.*[5] You say, "He was the Son of God. He already knew God's will." If we are following Christ and know even a little about the Bible, we have a pretty good feel for God's will. Which of the following requests would probably be God's will? "Dear God, please...

1. save my cousin Bill.
2. help me to be a good dad.
3. provide for me financially to get out of debt.
4. give me a new Mercedes.

Most of us would feel pretty confident about the first three being *God's will*. This fourth prayer may fall in the category of one of those *wrong motive* kinds of prayers.[6] What if asking for a new Mercedes would be something we are asking selfishly or would be bad for us? Is not God able to withhold something that might be detrimental or even better, reveal to us the selfishness of our hearts? He's a perfect Father. I'm an imperfect father and yet I knew better than to give my young children ice cream just before dinner, even though they were asking. To camp on this same analogy, the older they got the less they began to ask for ice cream before dinner because they began to understand my will. I'm also quite sure my children received many things from me simply because they asked. They probably would have received more had they been more bold to ask.

I used to be afraid to ask God for things fearing my response if I didn't get what I asked. I tended to play it safe so as not to be disappointed. That was before I understood how to pray prayers of lament when my petitions were not answered (I'll discuss this in the next chapter).

Jesus also taught us to ask repeatedly

In Luke 18 we find another prayer parable from Jesus. The persistent widow gets her request because she nags the unjust judge. *...because this widow keeps bothering me, I will see that she gets justice, so that she won't eventually wear me out with her coming!*[7] The point of the story is not subtle. It opens with *Then Jesus told his disciples a parable to show them that they should always pray and not give up.*[8] Don't be shy about asking until God answers (He may say "No"). *Ask* (keep on asking) *and it will be given you; seek* (keep on seeking) *and you will find; knock* (keep on knocking) *and the door will be opened to you.*

Recently, Janine was suffering from the flu. She had the classic symptoms—fever, chills, pain in her joints, and a nasty cough. As I've done for years for anyone I know who is sick, I placed my hands on her and asked God to heal her. Nothing happened. The next morning, I prayed again. She got worse. She went to work anyway and several other people at the church office gathered around her and prayed. She went home early and when I arrived that evening she was curled up on the couch under a blanket shivering with chills. Before I went to bed I prayed for her again. Shortly after I went to sleep she began to feel normal. She got up from the couch and went to work at the computer until late. The next morning she jumped right back into life and ministry full speed without a hint of sickness except for a lingering cough. Thank You, God!

Why should I ask? Doesn't God already know my needs?

Faith is in the asking. Jesus often did a strange thing when He encountered people with needs. He would ask what they wanted, even though it seemed obvious. Imagine having the power to heal and going up to a blind man and asking him: "What would you like me to do for you?"[9] (If he knew you had the power to make him see again). For some reason it was important for the blind man to say: *Teacher, I want to see.*[10] I don't fully understand it but there are plenty of examples in scripture of the importance of we humans asking God for His help. Faith is in the asking.

Can you imagine getting to heaven and hearing the Lord say: "I can't believe you asked me for so many things during your life on earth. You really bothered me by asking me save people, heal the sick, and bless people with finances. Of all the *gall!* I got so tired of you pleading with me for your children, your friends, your church. Hearing you say, 'Bless my life and make me fruitful really got annoying.'" I doubt it. What's more likely is to hear Him say: "Why didn't you ask Me for more? You had such a privilege—so much authority—so many opportunities to bring Me great glory by asking me for your needs and the needs of others?[11] It would have been my delight to give you whatever you had asked— Why didn't you go for it?"

I would rather be seen in the courts of heaven as a man of gall rather than someone who "had not because he asked not."[12]

B.H.A.P.

Several years ago I read a business book that spoke of the need for a company to have Big Hairy Audacious Goals.[13] But as I read I thought "What about the God-factor?" So I started coming up with Big Hairy Audacious Prayers, B.H.A.P. (pronounced "Beehap") for short. B.H.A.P. are prayers that only the living, powerful, awesome God that we know could possibly answer. They are not "guide the hands of the doctor" sort of prayers. They are more like *Send your healing power; may miraculous signs and wonders be done through the name of your holy servant Jesus*[14] sort of prayers. Our church is learning to pray B.H.A.P. prayers like: new followers of Jesus in our church (we are specific about the number we are asking for each year), more worshiping communities (churches and cell groups) in our city, church-planting movements in certain Muslim nations where we are sending teams.

I have a shelf full of my personal prayer journals containing hundreds of answered prayers. Several years ago during a one week period four different couples from our church came to me or called me grieving over their desire to have children. One had been trying for seven years, one six, and the other couples had been trying more than three years. With each I prayed a simple prayer and jotted their names in my prayer journal. Three of those couple now have two children and the fourth is expecting their third! Several have asked me to stop praying! I love it when God blesses people with children.

I could also show you numerous requests that I ve made that have yet to be answered or were answered "no." What about petitions that go unanswered? We'll tackle that subject in the next chapter.

Prayer Lab

1. In your next prayer time make a list of requests to present to God. Write them in your prayer journal if you are starting one.

2. Ask God for the things that you've written.

Chapter 12

Prayers of Lament

What do we do when we pray and nothing happens? I've experienced this many times. When we lived in Jogjakarta, Indonesia, I was asked to pray for a man who was critically ill. He lived in a *kampung,* a densely populated slum, where we had hopes of starting a new church. I thought, "What a great opportunity for God to demonstrate His power among Muslims by healing one of the prominent members of their community." As several of my believing friends and I entered the man's home I felt full of faith. We talked with the family a bit and made sure they were okay with Christians praying for this Muslim patriarch of the family. They welcomed our prayers. He was comatose, but from what we were sensing as we prayed, we felt confident God's Spirit was going to heal him. He stirred and then became coherent. We thanked God and made it clear that it was through the power and authority of Jesus Christ that this man was healed. But the next morning I got word that the man had died during the night! "God, you were seemingly able to heal him...couldn't You keep Him along alive enough to become a testimony to his community?" I pleaded. These disappointing experiences of unanswered prayer have caused me to lament.

If what you asked God for hasn't happened, you are in good company. Jesus' prayer to be delivered from the ordeal of the cross was denied.[1] Before that, He expressed a deep longing for the people of Jerusalem to accept Him and His message.[2] It didn't happen. What are we to do with the disappointment of unanswered prayer?

We must learn to lament in the presence of the Father. David was an expert "lamenter": *How long, O Lord? Will you forget me forever? How long will you hide your face from me? How long must I wrestle with my thoughts and every day have sorrow in my heart?* [3] Jesus quoted this prayer of lament of David: *My God, my God, why have you forsaken me? Why are you so far from saving me, so far from the words of my groaning? O my God, I cry out by day, but you do not answer, by night, and am not silent.*[4]

Here's how it works: We bring before God the longings of our heart. If nothing seems to happen, we don't give up. We keep asking. Then we hear a "no," or even more disappointing, no answer. It becomes increasingly apparent that it's not going to happen. The deadline for the payment has passed. The cancer patient we're praying for dies. The day of the decision has come, but still no sense of the Lord's leading. This is where we learn to come with gut-level honesty before the Lord.

In this kind of prayer we can freely express our

    Questions,

        grief,

            sorrow,

                disappointments,

                    even our *anger* to God!

David said: *I pour out my complaints before Him and tell Him all my troubles.*[5] Our relationship with God goes to a whole new level when we learn to lament before Him. God meets us in our sorrow and disappointments. Observe the pattern of David's prayers in the Psalms: He laments and then there's joy, trust and victory in his heart. Here's one of many examples from Psalm 74: *O God, why have you rejected us forever?...We see no miraculous signs as evidence that you will save us* (11 verses of this!). Then the tone changes: *You, O God, are my king from ages past...You split the sea by your strength and smashed the sea monsters' heads.*[6] We come to a place in which God comforts us and restores our trust in Him. But we must talk it through with Him, starting with a place of honesty in our hearts.

Let me give you a recent personal example of this kind of prayer. I was on a mission trip on a remote island in Indonesia. We had shared Christ with dozens of Muslims. Our prayer was for a key individual (*the man of peace*—see Luke 10) who would respond to the gospel and in turn influence his (or her) friends (Our B.H.A.P. was for God to help us initiate a church planting movement.). Several people had prayed to receive Christ, but none of them had seemed to be the key individual that could be part of a church planting movement. We were to leave that part of the island and head back to Bali in two days. I was watching the sun come up at a dock where fishing boats unload their nights catch. I prayed "Lord, it's not happening. I'm about to leave this place and I feel so fruitless. I feel like I've been fishing all night and haven't caught any fish. What's up with this?" I was in *lamenting mode.*

I turned around and there was a man standing behind me named Agus who had come to watch the sunrise. Agus turned out to be very interested in the gospel. So interested, he wanted to hear more. So we set an appointment to meet again later that morning. He didn't turn to Christ (while we were there) but he introduced me to Ibrahim, Yusuf, Aman, and Elias—all who listened intently to the Good News and prayed to receive Christ! Elias turned out to be a very influential man among the shrimp farmers of the area. We believe he is the *man of peace* for whom we had been praying.

Like the disciples of old, Jesus told me where to cast my net.[7] God meets us in our disappointment, even when things don't turn out as we had hoped.

Prayers of lament sound a lot like complaining or whining. But it's much more appropriate (and effective) to whine and complain with God than with people. We do so respectfully, with submission to Him as the all-knowing, all-wise God. However, He doesn't seem to be bothered by His people who don't take "no" easily. He's okay with us asking, "Why not?" Here's one of my favorite examples of a good lamenter:

In those days Hezekiah became ill and was at the point of death. The prophet Isaiah son of Amoz went to him and said, "This is what the Lord says: Put your house in order, because you are going to die; you will not recover."

Hezekiah turned his face to the wall and prayed to the Lord, "Remember, O Lord , how I have walked before you faithfully and with wholehearted devotion and have done what is good in your eyes."

And Hezekiah wept bitterly.

Before Isaiah had left the middle court, the word of the Lord came to him: *"Go back and tell Hezekiah, the leader of my people, 'This is what the Lord, the God of your father David, says: I have heard your prayer and seen your tears; I will heal you. On the third day from now you will go up to the temple of the Lord. I will add fifteen years to your life. And I will deliver you and this city from the hand of the king of Assyria. I will defend this city for my sake and for the sake of my servant David.'"*

Then Isaiah said, "Prepare a poultice of figs." They did so and applied it to the boil, and he recovered.[8]

The rest of the story of the *kampung* in Jogjakarta, Indonesia, is this: I followed up with the family of the Muslim man who died after we had prayed. They weren't bitter or cynical. They were sincerely thankful I had cared enough to pray. By the time we left Jogjakarta a cell group had been formed in that *kampung* and there were nearly two dozen new followers of Jesus.

Not all of my prayers of lament turn out to have a happy ending. Some couples I've prayed for to conceive are still without children. Some terminal illnesses resulted in death, not miraculous healing. Some bold requests for financial needs weren't answered on the date I had requested. There are prayers I've prayed for my family and the church that I serve that seem like they will never be answered, or like the answer is "no." I've been asking for the people in my neighborhood to come to Christ. So far, There's not been one new convert. I've been disappointed in God on many occasions, but trust, confidence and intimacy is restored when I come to Him gut-honest.

Prayer Lab

1. Are there things that you've been asking God to do that haven't or apparently won't happen?
2. Are there ways that you've felt hurt, disappointed, or even angry with God?
3. Tell Him about it. Be honest with Him. You can be real with reverence and respect.

Chapter 13

Prayers of Trust

George Mueller left behind an amazing legacy, more than starting and leading one of the largest orphanages in history—The Orphan House of Bristol, England. He also modeled a life of prayer that was truly amazing. He refused to solicit funds for the overwhelming financial challenge of housing, clothing, and feeding hundreds and eventually thousands of orphans in 19th century England. He and his staff simply "prayed in" all of their financial needs for every child, every day for more than 50 years! On many occasions there was absolutely no food or money to buy food at 11 AM, and by noon there was food enough for every orphan! Never did any of the children under his care go without a meal. His journal records 30,000 such answers to prayer! How did he have the faith to see so many answers to prayer? He mastered the art of praying the promises of God.

He made it a practice while praying to read or quote God's promises found in scripture.

He would pray promises like, "God, you see the needs of these children. They are not my children. You are *the father to the fatherless.*"[1]

"And are You not *their helper?*"[2]

"And didn't You say You *would supply all of our needs according to your riches in mercy?*"[3]

Mueller himself taught that it wasn't about convincing God to act when he prayed in this manner. It was more for the benefit of *his faith* that he learned to pray God's promises. The faith to believe God for that which we are asking is bolstered through our expressions of trust and confidence in the promises of God and His character.

Writers of the Bible often expressed their trust in God by praying promises about His character:

I cry out to God Most High, to God who will fulfill his purpose for me. He will send help from heaven to save me. My God will send forth his unfailing love and faithfulness.[4]

I trust in God, so why should I be afraid?[5]

When Daniel was deeply troubled by the news of the pending destruction of Jerusalem, he fasted and prayed. Notice how he begins his prayer: *O Lord, you are a great and awesome God! You always fulfill your promises of unfailing love to those who love you and keep your commands.*[6]

Communicating trust in God and His promises not only builds our faith, it enhances our intimacy with Him.

You may feel a deep level trust in God but that trust needs to be expressed and communicated. There's something affirming, intimate, and deeply personal when we express our trust in someone. When my wife looks me in the eye and says: "I trust you in this Ron," I feel humbled by her trust and so grateful for the intimacy in our relationship. As my relationship with the Lord has matured over the years I find myself often telling Him that I trust Him. *My heart is confident in you, O God.*[7]

Imagine yourself being the parent of a teenage son. One day he calls you and says: "Mom, I just wanted to say I really trust your counsel, direction, and the wisdom you've spoken into my life. You have helped steer me on a good course." Or, "Dad, I'm so thankful for the way you've provided for my needs. You have sacrificed consistently to meet my physical needs, and it gives me confidence that I don't have to be worried about my future. Thank you."

And then, he stops there. You weren't being buttered up for a, "By the way, can I borrow the car Friday night?" There is no request for money, just a sincere expression of his trust in you. After you pick yourself up off the floor you would probably feel very loved and appreciated by this child.

Who is God?

"What do you believe about God?" Someone challenged me with this question recently. I wrote in my prayer journal: "I *believe* You love me very much. I *believe* You want me to bear much fruit—even more than I want to be fruitful. I *believe* You are doing all You can to shape me, train me, and equip me to bring You much glory. I *believe* that Your hand is on my life in ways that I will know only in heaven." There were about two more pages of these statements of belief. To reflect on what you believe about God is a powerful devotional exercise.

Try this: next time you sense a need for God's help in a decision spend some time acknowledging God as your Shepherd, Counselor and Guide. Read the promises you can find in scripture for guidance and turn them into prayers of trust. Your faith will soar. The more I know God the more I find myself praying prayers of trust for every area of my life.

Who are you?

Not only do we declare the trustworthiness of God and His promises, we can affirm what God says about us. You can celebrate the truth of what He says about you.

I love the scene from "The Lion King" where Simba's father tells him from above, "You have forgotten who you are." Simba is a fierce king, yet he was hiding in fear from the responsibilities of his domain and was eating bugs with his new friends, a warthog and a merekat. While I can't endorse all the theology of that movie, I can say forgetting who you are always leads to a defilement of your glory and destiny in God.

Another movie, "Kingdom of Heaven," has a great scene in it when Balian, the newly knighted defender of Jerusalem, surveys the city's defenses and fighters and realizes they are not ready for a full-scale attack. A scornful cleric asks him, "How will you defend Jerusalem without knights? We need knights!" Balian then turns to a young servant boy and commands him to kneel, with all the other young men of Jerusalem. He publicly knights hundreds of them at the same time. They all rise with a glimmer of courage in their eyes and the cleric protests, "Who do you think you are? Will you change the world? Will calling a man a knight make him fight better?" Balian looks the doubting cleric in the eyes and answers a defiant, "Yes." The newly knighted young men look at the old man with disdain and you can see a fighting spirit in their eyes. They now know who they are, and they are now willing to fight like knights.

Are you fighting the good fight from a base of identity of who God says you are? Several years ago I began a list entitled: "Who God says I am." I transfer this list to each new journal. It's a work in progress. Often, when I'm being barraged with the condemning lies of the enemy, I pray through this list:

By the death and resurrection of Jesus Christ and the sanctifying work of the Holy Spirit I am:

1. Blessed with every spiritual blessing in Christ Jesus (Ephesians 1:3)
2. Chosen in Him before the creation of the world (Ephesians 1:4; 1 Peter 2:9)

3. Made holy in Jesus Christ (1 Corinthians 1:2)
4. A son of God (Romans 8:15)
5. A slave to righteousness (Romans 6:18)
6. Free from the controlling power of sin (Romans 6:6-7)
7. God's workmanship—His masterpiece (Ephesians 2:10)
8. Destined to do good works which God has prepared for me (Ephesians 2:10)
9. Near to God, by the blood of Jesus Christ (Ephesians 2:13)
10. God's possession—I belong to Him (2 Corinthians 5:14-15; 1 Peter 2:9; 1 Timothy 6:11)
11. A new person/creation (2 Corinthians 5:17)
12. Dead to the flesh—the old pattern of living (Romans 6:3,7)
13. More than a conqueror through Him who loves me (Romans 8:37)
14. God's witness—even to the ends of the earth (Acts 1:8)
15. God's friend (John 15:15-16)
16. Able to do all things through Him who gives me strength (Philippians :13)
17. Loved by God—the object of His compassion (John 16:27; Romans 8:37)
18. Righteous—in right standing with God (Romans 5:19)
19. Not of this world—I am a foreigner, an alien (1 Peter 1:17)
20. A priest (1 Peter 2:9)
21. A member of His household—His family (1 Peter 2:9-10)
22. The salt of the earth (Matthew 5:13)
23. The light of the world (Matthew 5:14)
24. Complete—I have everything I need for living a godly life (2 Peter 1:3)
25. Able to say "no" to temptation, ungodliness, and worldly passions (1 Corinthians 10:13; Titus 2:12)
26. An overcomer—because greater is He who is in me than he who is in the world (1 John 4:4; 5:4)
27. A fisher of men (Matthew 4:19)

28. A member of the body of Christ (1 Corinthians 12:13,27)
29. A slave to Jesus Christ (Jude 1)
30. An ambassador of Christ Jesus (2 Corinthians 5:20)
31. Alive with life that is truly life (Romans 6:11; Ephesians 2:4-5)
32. Seated with Christ in heavenly places (Ephesians 2:6)
33. Given a new heart— a good and noble heart. (Ezekiel 36:26; Luke 8:15)

These are not promises for the spiritual elite who have conjured them up in a state of spiritual ecstasy off on a mountain top somewhere. These are God's everyday promises describing all of us who have experienced the transforming work of salvation through faith in Jesus Christ. Next time you are being slimed by the enemy or you just feel discouraged, pray these promises out loud. Plant your feet in your true identity, and your heart will be lifted to new heights of intimacy with the Father.

Prayer Lab

1. Think of some promises you remember from the Word (if you can't think of any, start with the ones above). Express your trust in God to fulfill these promises for you.

2. Start your own list of "What God Says About Me" as you come across these promises in God's Word.

Chapter 14

Kingdom Warfare Prayers

I was recently in a meeting with a group of elders from a dynamic, thriving church. The senior pastor shared with us a dream he had the night before that he sensed was from the Lord. Through his dream he and the elders understood the church to be coming under attack through a strategic plan of the enemy. We launched into Kingdom Warfare Prayer. It was intense. It was loud. We had our Bibles in hand, praying scriptures from the Bible. At times we were all praying at the same time. Yet there was an amazing sense of unity in our contending together for God's purposes against the one who would seek to destroy the church. We felt like we were like Gandalf in *Lord of the Rings* when he held up his staff and told the Balrog: "You shall not pass." We were wrestling the powers of darkness with *God's mighty weapons, not merely worldly weapons, to knock down the devil's strongholds.*[1] The breakthrough we experienced after about 45 minutes of this kind of prayer was palpable. The heaviness lifted. The atmosphere of the meeting became almost giddy. Something had happened in the spirit realm.

This is *not* the kind of prayer I experienced in church when I was a kid. For me everything about church, especially prayer, was anything *but* warlike. The Jesus I learned about in Sunday School was more like Mr. Rogers than William Wallace. Prayer was for the women and children, or passive men. It was what one did if he or she were helpless or when all else failed. "O well, at least we can pray." Prayer was all about surrender, not going to battle. For a ten-year-old boy whose aspiration was be a warrior, I was not very excited about learning to pray. I couldn't have been more wrong!

What does a Kingdom Warfare Prayer look like? It's authoritative.

I learned to recite the Lord's Prayer: *May your Kingdom come, may your will be done* [2] as if I were making a birthday wish or in the tone of "May your days be happy and bright." I have learned to pray this statement with much more authority. In the original language it's a command that should be translated more like: *Kingdom of God come, will of God be done.* It's as if we are speaking into existence God's kingly reign. This kind of prayer is *fighting the fight of faith* [3] until God's will becomes a reality.

It's vital to understand that we are not using *our* authority. We don't even *take authority* in prayer. We exercise the authority of Jesus Christ. God has given Jesus all authority in heaven and on earth,[4] and in turn, Jesus has given us authority due to our relationship with Him.[5]

In one sense when we pray we are joining Jesus Christ in His battle against Satan as what we *bind on earth will be (will **have been**) bound in heaven, whatever you loose on earth, will be (will **have been**) loosed in heaven.*[6] Just like a traffic cop exercises the authority given to him to direct eighteen-wheelers to stop or to go, we are praying under God's authority.

I love praying with people who understand prayer in this way. One such man in our church is Dick Rolph. Dick recently told me of being stirred by the Spirit to pray for a particular African country. At first, he wasn't even sure which country! After an hour or so the word Niger came to mind. He wasn't aware of any particular crisis taking place there but he prayed for hours sensing that the future of this nation was in the balance. Eventually the battle waned, and he was released from this burden of intercession. Several days later it was reported in the news that the government of Niger had just successfully held a peaceful election in which the political party that most protected human rights prevailed.

It's aggressive and combative.

Sometimes prayer is like a wrestling match. *For our struggle* (a hand-to-hand battle) *is not against flesh and blood, but against the rulers, against the authorities, against the powers of this dark world and against the spiritual forces of evil in the heavenly realms.*[7] It should be no surprise that when the apostle Paul, fully understanding this battle we face with the spiritual forces of evil, tells us to put on the armor that God provides and *pray.* Prayer (along with the sword of the Spirit) is our offensive weapon: *And pray in the Spirit on all occasions with all kinds of prayers and requests. With this in mind, be alert and always keep on praying for all the saints.*[8]

Weak, wimpy, or even self-centered prayer won't cut it in battle. I love John Piper's analogy of prayer. Prayer can be likened to communication with headquarters in which a soldier on the battle front uses his walkie-talkie to call in fire power to take out an enemy position. Piper carries the analogy even further: Too often we see prayer as an intercom system which we use for calling in more comforts in the den of our homes (or the cabins in our boats)![9]

It declares God's truth to counter the lies of the enemy.

When the enemy came at Jesus, he quoted the Word of God.[10] The only weapon in the armor we are told to wear into battle is our sword—*the sword of the Spirit, which is the Word of God.*[11] Satan's favorite strategy in getting us is deception. He plants lies in our thoughts; often, those condemning lies harass us until we lose heart. I've learned that there's incredible power declaring God's truth in times of intense warfare.

At times, this kind of prayer addresses the powers of darkness.

This will be a stretch for some of you, but there are times that it's appropriate to speak to the powers of darkness in Kingdom Warfare Prayer. "We now command every vile, unclean spirit that may be present in this room to flee. Return now to the place from which you came. By the authority of Jesus Christ every immoral act that's ever taken place here will have no effect on us—be cleansed by the blood of Jesus. Jesus Christ is Lord of this hotel room." This was the kind of prayer we prayed when traveling throughout the islands of Bali, Lombok, and Sumbawa in Indonesia last summer. We stayed in 32 different locations, many of which had probably never been visited by Christians. I'm not often very discerning of evil spirits. But even I have sensed the presence of dark spirits in $5 per night "hotels" in some of these isolated places. On occasion, I have forgotten to "clean the room" and have experienced demonic dreams, dark moods, or even strange illnesses.

One note of caution is that there's a word for Christians who always address Satan or evil spirits in their "prayers"—weird. We don't go around picking street fights with evil spirits. They will raise their ugly heads when we advance God's kingdom through our witness to the lost. We speak to them only when necessary.

Here's an example of a Kingdom Warfare Prayer I came across recently in John Eldredge's book *Waking the Dead*:

"Jesus, I also receive You as my authority and rule, my everlasting victory over Satan and his kingdom, and I receive all the work and triumph of Your ascension, whereby Satan has been judged and cast down...I bring Your authority and Your kingdom rule over my life, my family, my household, and my domain.

"And now I bring the fullness of Your work—Your cross, resurrection, and ascension—against Satan, against his kingdom, and against all his emissaries and all their work warring against me and my domain. Greater is He who is in me than he who is in the world. Christ has given me authority to overcome all the power of the Evil One, and I claim that authority now over and against every enemy, and I banish them in the name of Jesus Christ. Holy Spirit apply to me (my wife and my children) the fullness of the work of the ascension of Jesus Christ for me. I receive it with thanks and give it total claim to my life."[12]

Prayer Lab

1. What are specific ways you have sensed the Enemy's attack against you personally? (Sickness, fear, lust, discouragement, bitterness, unbelief, etc.?)

2. Turn Psalms 6:10; 23:5; 44:1-7; 1 John 4:4; Romans 8:37 into prayers, naming your enemies and reciting God's promises to defeat them.

3. Pray out loud with faith and intensity.

Chapter 15

Praying the Bible

My stereotype of seminary professors was rocked the first time I heard Dr. Everett Harrison pray. It was my first week of class at Fuller Seminary, and he opened in prayer for his class on the book of Acts. In his soft-spoken, grandfatherly voice he led us to the throne with such authority and power, tears came to my eyes. It wasn't one of those lengthy, religious, boring prayers. It was like a smart bomb that found its way into the bunker of my soul. The key was that He prayed God's Word. To be more specific, he turned several key verses from the Book of Acts into his personal longings for us budding theologians. I made it a point never to be late for Dr. Harrison's class. The inspiration of those biblical prayers alone was worth the price of the class.

The prayers of the Bible

There are far more prayers in the Word than you can imagine. Herbert Lockyer in *All the Prayers of the Bible* has identified over 175 prayers in the New Testament alone!

You've probably prayed the 23rd Psalm or the Lord's Prayer. Have you ever come across this one?

O Sovereign Lord! You have made the heavens and the earth by your great power. Nothing is too hard for you. You are loving and kind to thousands... You are the great and powerful God, the

Lord Almighty. You have all wisdom and do great and mighty miracles.[1]

It's found in Jeremiah. There are prayers like this one tucked away throughout the Bible. They are easy to personalize by simply praying them out loud. Most of the Psalms are prayers originally put to music. There's power in making these prayers your own.

My personal favorites are Paul's apostolic prayers. I've committed several of them to memory and have prayed them for many years. For example:

I keep asking that the God of our Lord Jesus Christ, the glorious Father, may give you the Spirit of wisdom and revelation, so that you may know him better.

I pray also that the eyes of your heart may be enlightened in order that you may know the hope to which he has called you, the riches of his glorious inheritance in the saints, and his incomparably great power for us who believe.[2]

I pray that out of his glorious riches he may strengthen you with power through his Spirit in your inner being, so that Christ may dwell in your hearts through faith. And I pray that you, being rooted and established in love, may have power, together with all the saints, to grasp how wide and long and high and deep is the love of Christ, and to know this love that surpasses knowledge—that you may be filled to the measure of all the fullness of God.[3]

Turning other scriptures into prayers

Great stories of the Bible, teachings, admonitions, prophecies, and even proverbs can be transformed into personal prayers. I have found that there's something from nearly every chapter of the Bible that's "prayer-worthy." Here's how it works:

1. **Pick a chapter, any chapter.** Ideally, you are reading through the Bible in your devotional time. For example, say you are reading Titus, chapter 1 (What I read today). Read it.

2. **Look for things that you could turn into prayers of thanksgiving.** For example: *I (Paul) have been sent to bring faith to those God has chosen and to teach them the truth that shows them how to live godly lives* (verse 1). "Thank you Lord that You have sent people my way who told me and showed me the gospel. Thank you for choosing me. Thank you for the great teaching I've had to help me to live a godly life. Thank you that I have been given this same awesome privilege: To be sent to *bring faith to those You have chosen.*" Notice I personalize it. It becomes a prayer of the heart.

3. **Now, find things in this chapter that speak of the character and goodness of God.** For example, Paul calls God his *Savior* in verse 3. I wrote in my journal: "I praise You God for being my Savior." In verse 4 he speaks of *God the Father and Christ Jesus* as the giver of *grace and peace.* "I love You so much God for giving me grace and peace." "Praise You, Jesus Christ: You are my grace and peace." Creative, fresh prayers of adoration and love for our Triune God will began to flow out of what you read.

4. **You may sense the conviction of the Holy Spirit** through what you find in the scriptures you are reading. You read: *He (an elder) must lead a devout and disciplined life* (verse 8). And you realize how long it's been since you've exercised. Confess your lack of discipline and pray prayers of sincere repentance.

5. **There are many ways we can commit ourselves to God** on a new level through prayers of submission we can pray from this chapter. For example, "I offer myself to You today, Lord, as Your *slave*" (verse 1). "I commit myself to You *to live a devout and disciplined life*" (verse 8).

6. **You could form at least a dozen prayers of petition from this chapter.** For example, you could go down the list of character traits of an elder (verses 6-9) and ask God to help you "live out" these attributes (even if you are not an elder).

7. **Pray these same qualities for the elders and pastors** of your church. This could move into a powerful time of intercession. You could easily pray several of the promises, truths, or insights from this chapter for the nonbelievers in your network of influence.

8. **The passage you encounter may evoke prayers of trust or kingdom authority prayers**—or any other *kind of prayer* we've discussed.

I have actually spent several days "praying through" Titus 1. I'm also currently reading Ezekiel. (I usually read through both the Old and New Testaments at the same time.) So far, I'm finding it more challenging to find prayer inspiration in Ezekiel than in Titus; but the next time I pray through Ezekiel, it may be more of what God is saying to me at the time. It's a dynamic process.

I have a friend named John "Bud" Brown who has served as a missionary in Indonesia for more than 35 years. Early in his missionary career on a trip to Kalimantan (Borneo) he began the discipline of reading huge chunks of the scripture daily. He finished the whole Bible in 40 days and started over. He has repeated this process over 200 times and counting! I once asked him: "Does it ever getting boring to you?" His response: "Are you kidding? It's like commuting through the countryside with the most beautiful scenery imaginable. Every day you observe something new and beautiful along the way."

There's endless "prayer fodder" throughout the Bible. You will never exhaust the ways you can pray scripture. Martin Luther said: "If you picture the Bible to be a mighty tree and every word a little branch, I have shaken every one of these branches because I wanted to know what it was and what it meant." Imagine how rich God's Word would become to you if you not only shake but prayed "every little branch." Imagine how rich your prayer life would be if you turned everything you read in the Bible into a personal prayer. You would pray with greater authority and confidence. Prayer would never be routine or boring.

Prayer Lab

1. If you are reading in a specific place in the Bible, walk through steps 1-5 in this chapter.

2. If you are not reading the Bible through in a systematic way, start with the first chapter of Genesis, Psalms, Matthew, or John. Pray through the chapter using the 5 steps outlined in this chapter.

Chapter 16

Prayers Worth Repeating

Many prayers are worth re-praying. The most obvious ones—the most authoritative, are found in God's Word (see Chapter 15). There are also time-tested prayers prayed by others who lived in centuries past. There's power and life in some of these prayers. These are people who are more articulate than us who may have ways of praying from which we have much to learn. There are also prayers that come from our heart that we find ourselves praying over and over again. We can record them, and they can become powerful weapons in our prayer arsenal.

Borrowed prayers
Check out these prayers:

"May God the Father who made us bless us.

May God the Son send his healing among us.

May God the Holy Spirit move within us and give us,

Eyes to see with, ears to hear with,

and hands that your work might be done.

May we walk and preach the word of God to all.

May the angel of peace watch over us and lead us,

At last by God's grace to the Kingdom."

—St. Dominic 1170-1221

"Dearest Lord,

Teach me to be generous.

Teach me to serve you as you deserve;

To give, and not count the cost;

to fight and not to heed the wounds;

to labor, and not seek to rest,

to give myself, and not ask for reward,

except the reward that I am doing your will."

—St. Ignatius of Loyola 1491-1556

Other great prayers from past century devotional masters are found in:

The Book of Common Prayer
Celtic Prayers from Ion, by J. Philip Newell
Devotional Classics: Selected Readings for Individuals and Groups, by Richard J. Foster

There are plenty of contemporary prayer books and prayer guides on the shelves at Christian bookstores. My friend Steve Hawthorne provides an excellent prayer guide for the forty days leading up to Palm Sunday called *Seek God for the City.*

Crafted Prayers

Crafted Prayers are prayers that we compose and repeat. (I'm indebted to Graham Cooke for this prayer discipline.) Here's an example of a prayer that I "crafted" on April 2, 2003. It's a *Prayer for Boldness in Sharing My Faith*. It goes like this:

Father, I thank You for the awesome privilege of:
* having been told the gospel
* experiencing its transforming power
* being a witness to the reality of who You are and what You can do in the lives of men and women
* being called to partner with You as You reconcile people to Yourself

Please...
* Love people into Your kingdom through me.
* Stir me with compassion for the lost.
* Help me to truly care about the people I encounter today.
* Give me at least one opportunity to tell someone about Your kindness, Your mercy, Your purpose — longing for their life.
* Give me boldness, through Your Spirit, to speak up.
* Enable me to speak to their heart needs — to communicate effectively your ability to meet those needs.
* Give me the ability to invite them to put their trust in You for salvation (in a tactful manner).

By your grace I choose to:
* do the work of an evangelist
* be a winsome, contagious witness
* actively share my faith
* sow the seeds of the gospel liberally everywhere I go

I've prayed this prayer dozens of times since then. It's been through several revisions. It now more expresses my passionate longings. Its also more biblical than my original version. God seems to be answering this cry of my heart. In my own strength I am timid and reserved when it comes to sharing my faith. But I actually feel myself being transformed into a bold witness for Christ the longer I pray this prayer.

What about spontaneity? Doesn't reading and repeating written prayers take away from personal, heartfelt, on-the-spot, sincere prayers? No way! First of all, we personalize all of the prayers that we choose to repeat. The prayers that we create ourselves (crafted prayers) are birthed from the depths of our souls. There can be a power, beauty, and precision of thought expressed in our crafted prayers. It's like writing poetry to your sweetheart as opposed to depending on your extemporaneous expression of a stream of consciousness. (To carry the analogy further, a poem that you write, however clumsy and awkward, would probably have a greater impact on him or her than something composed by Shakespeare.)

Secondly, when you repeat a crafted prayer, there is freedom to expound on what you've written. It's like giving a speech from a prepared outline. Sometimes, the most profound thing you might say is when you veer off from your notes. But it's good to have notes.

Here's the process of crafting your own prayers:

- Identify a prayer need (love, joy, victory, faith, etc.)
- Compile as many scriptures as you can find that relate to this need
- Meditate on these truths/promises
- Write out a prayer
- Pray it for a season
- Re-craft it as needed
- P. U. S. H. - Pray Until Something Happens

Imagine yourself longing for greater joy in your life. You've prayed for it. But it's been hit or miss—mostly when you are battling depression. Then, you compile a list of scriptures that speak of the promise of joy for those who know Jesus Christ. In your prayer times you read over these promises and begin to turn them into personal prayers. You write out a prayer that incorporates these promises. Imagine the expansion of inexpressible, supernatural, eternal joy that begins to grow inside you as you daily express these longings to God in prayer. It may take a year or ten years. But transformation is inevitable.

Prayer Lab

1. Pick out a prayer that others have prayed. Pray it a few times. How did it feel?

2. Craft your own prayer. Work through steps 1-4 mentioned in this chapter. Don't worry about perfecting it. You will probably revise it over time. Pray it today and tomorrow.

Chapter 17

Praying With
Our Spirit

I spent some time praying with a friend this morning. He's facing a tough decision. We thanked God for the ways He's been working in my friend's life. We prayed some of the promises of God's Word. I asked God to do some very specific things in his life (petition prayers). After about twenty minutes I ran out of things to say, so I began to pray in tongues. I wouldn't have done this had I thought this kind of prayer would offend him or weird him out (He was praying in tongues too!). Something was communicated to God: there was some kind of spiritual release that took place as we prayed in our spiritual language. Neither he nor I understood what we were saying, but God did.

When the Apostle Paul prayed this way he said he was *praying with his spirit*.[1] He didn't understand what he was saying but his spirit (his inner being) was communicating with God. The Greek word used for this kind of prayer is *glossolalia*—translated *speaking in tongues*. Paul listed it as one of the spiritual gifts. Paul took pains in his first letter to the church at Corinth to explain its proper use because they had abused it in their public worship gatherings. Speaking in tongues was a badge of spirituality for some of the Corinthians. You would think with such a distorted view (a pseudo-spirituality associated with this gift) Paul would downplay its value. On the contrary he says speaking in tongues:

- Is a form of prayer—*anyone who speaks in a tongue does not speak to men but to God* [2]
- Builds oneself up spiritually[3]

Paul boasts that he personally speaks in tongues even more than the tongues-crazed Corinthians.[4] He doesn't use this gift in the public worship gathering (except when it's interpreted). He uses it in private prayer—a lot. He even sings *with his spirit.*[5] His prayer life is a mixture of prayers that he understands and prayers that he doesn't understand.[6] He knows that when someone is speaking in tongues he can be *praising God with his spirit.*[7] No wonder Paul says: *I would like every one of you to speak in tongues.*[8]

Some who have yet to experience this form of prayer may be fearful of losing control, coming under some mystical spell that may be demonic (or at least totally weird). Speaking in tongues is not uncontrolled babble. The Spirit doesn't zap us and we wake up speaking in tongues. That's why *ecstatic utterance* is a poor translation of this phenomena. I exercise my will to start and stop speaking in tongues. The Holy Spirit enables me to communicate with God in this way but I choose to exercise this gift that He has given me.

What are we saying when we pray in our prayer language?

Paul says he who is praying in tongues *utters mysteries with his spirit.*[9] No one knows exactly what they are saying except we or someone with whom we are praying receives the interpretation. There are occasions that someone's prayer language happens to be a living language understood by someone who happens to be nearby. That's what happened on the Day of Pentecost. Once, after speaking in one of our church plants in an isolated Javanese village up in the mountains, one of our team members came to me and said: "Pak (Mr.) Ron, you have to hear this." She took me to

From Duty To Delight

the back of the crowd gathered up front praying. There was a sweet old lady praying prayers of adoration and praise in perfect English. After the service I tried to strike up a conversation with her in English. She was clueless. Her spiritual language happened to be English. (Please don't ask me to explain this: I just know that one's prayer language is occasionally a living language.)

On the Day of Pentecost the content of the spirit-prayers of the 120 was declarations of *the wonders of God*.[10] In other words, they were expressing what their spirits felt of the beauty and majesty of God. Paul says he is *praising God with his spirit* and expressing gratitude[11] when he prays in tongues.

I'm confident that some of our prayers in our spirit are prayers of intercession. The *groans words can't express*[12] could be Spirit-led and Spirit-empowered prayers on our behalf or prayers for others in need of which we had no prior or specific knowledge. When Janine was thirteen years old she was awakened in the middle of the night with a distinct impression that she should pray in the Spirit. She slipped out of bed and obediently launched out in her prayer language sensing this overwhelming heaviness of a struggle in the Spirit on behalf of someone in need. After a while the name Anderson came to mind. (No, this was not the *Mr. Anderson* of the Matrix—this was decades before the movie came out.) Eventually the burden lifted, and she fell back asleep. She had no idea for whom she was praying until two years later at youth conference the speaker was a missionary named Jim Anderson serving in India. On the very night the Holy Spirit had stirred her for intercession he was involved in a serious accident while operating heavy equipment in which he lost his arm. (Given the time difference it was daytime in India.) By his own testimony, God miraculously spared his life through the prayers of people, including a thirteen year old girl in Austin, Texas.

Why risk the weirdness?

Some of my evangelical friends tell me: "I pray just fine without this gift." Obviously, one can have Spirit-led, Spirit-empowered prayers without the gift of tongues. Some have been taught Paul's personal use of this form of prayer and his explicit teaching about *glossalalia* is inappropriate for today. Like it or not our experience affects our theology. For we who pray in tongues it's easy to understand why Paul would say *I would like every one of you to speak in tongues.*[13] There's a level of intimacy that we engage in through our prayer language we don't experience when forming our own words to pray. Somehow, the part of me that connects with God (my spirit) is strengthened and fortified. How? I admit, at times I feel rather foolish pacing on my backyard deck talking to a God I don't see in a language I don't understand. But something is happening beyond my intellect. My heart is being transformed into some kind of Superman, Spiderman, or the Incredible Hulk in the Spirit.

Is tongues for everyone?

Paul asks the rhetorical question: *Do all speak in tongues?*[14] The answer he expects from the reader is *no!* But he does say he wished all of the people in the church at Corinth spoke in tongues, at least, in their private prayer times at home.

Let's get personal. What if you are asking: "Is speaking in tongues for me?" Do you find your own words can't fully express what you long to communicate to God? Why not seek this gift? We're told to *eagerly desire spiritual gifts.*[15] It *is*, after all, a form of prayer that strengthens our inner being. It's not weird. Not only did the Apostle Paul pray this way, but millions of Christians around the world find added life in their times with God while praying in their spiritual language.[16]

Prayer Lab

1. If you speak in tongues, take at least 20 minutes of your next prayer time and pray in the Spirit. Monitor your spirit. Do you feel closer to God and strengthened in your inner person? If so, keep it up for a couple of weeks and see what happens.

2. If this in new to you, read *The Beauty of Spiritual Language* by Jack Hayford. Follow his instructions in ways you can experience this powerful gift.

Chapter 18

A Life-Giving Hour
Spent with God

Let's get really practical here. You are motivated to spend an hour in focused, meaningful interaction with God tomorrow morning. You set the alarm early enough to give yourself plenty of time, keeping in mind all the other things you need to do to get out the door to head to work or school or get your kids up and going, etc. What do you actually *do* during that hour?

1. **Pull out your journal and make a "thankful list"** (see Chapter 7). Jot down things that come to mind that have happened during the last 24 hours for which you are grateful, blessings of God in your life, etc. Now verbalize this list in a sincere prayer.

2. **Read over a couple of chapters from the Bible**, ideally including a Psalm and at least one chapter from the New Testament. Look for verses in these chapters that you can turn into prayers of adoration and praise (see Chapter 8). Write them out in your prayer journal or simply pray them out loud. Sing one of your favorite hymns or worship songs to the Lord or simply declare some of the names and attributes of God or Jesus.

3. Is the Holy Spirit convicting you (Chapter 9) or speaking to you about ways you need to respond to what you have read? Repent and receive His forgiveness if that is necessary.

4. Pray prayers of submission/surrender/commitment (Chapter 10) from what you have just read or from other verses that come to mind. Commit the day's schedule to the Lord, along with anything else that comes to mind.

5. Express to the Lord the longings of your heart for yourself or others (Chapter 11). List them in your journal and then verbalize them. Often, I turn what I read in the Word into a prayer of petition. For example, this morning I prayed for Psalm 112. "Lord, please:
- Fill me with *joy* as one who fears You (verse 1)
- Make my children successful (verse 2)
- Send Your light in the places of my life where I sense the darkness overwhelming me (verse 4)
- May I leave a legacy of righteousness (verse 6). (My list included about five more requests.)

How long will this take? I practice these disciplines daily and I rarely get finished with these first 5 in less than an hour. I don't time myself or even think: "I need to make sure and pray every kind of prayer." I just go with the flow. But even if you gave yourself 7 minutes per *kind of prayer* plus the 10 minutes or so it will take to read 3-4 chapters from the Bible—you're talking 45 minutes! You could easily take another 15 minutes praying one or more of the other kinds of prayer that we've addressed:
- **Prayers of Lament** (Chapter 12)
- **Declarations of Trust** (Chapter 13)
- **Kingdom Warfare Prayers** (Chapter 14)

- **Borrowed Prayers or Crafted Prayers** (Chapter 16)
- **Prayer in the Spirit** (Chapter 17)

Try this once and you will find that this is the most meaningful hour of your day. Begin to incorporate these kinds of prayers into your life-style on a daily basis and your spiritual life will soar. You will feel more of God's presence in your life. You'll enjoy greater intimacy with Him. You will have more joy. The trials and burdens of your life will seem less significant. You will be more loving. You will walk in the Spirit more consistently. You will live out who you truly *are* in Him. Your faith will flourish and those closest to you will say, "What's happened to you?" Most importantly, you will bring greater glory to God through the fruit of your life.

Another thing you will find—*prayer will not be boring for you.* Taking an hour or more to pray like this has yet to become a dull routine or religious duty for me, even after thirty years! There's structure but I'm never bound to a rigid set of prayers. Even my crafted prayers are fresh and life-giving every time I recite them. (I never simply read them—I always expound on them.) The fact is that *no two prayer times are alike.* It's like a conversation with someone you're really close to—it's never scripted. There's a dynamic flow of give and take, of speaking and responding...and listening. Most days, either quickly or laboriously, I eventually experience God's life-giving presence. *It's so worthy of my time and efforts to meet Him.*

Chapter 19

Unscheduled Prayers

"Help us, Jesus!" That's all I could manage to say when a truck I was attempting to pass swerved into my lane as we neared a village on the island of Java. It was a moment of terror as the Nissan Patrol I was driving went into an uncontrolled spin and began to roll over. Two of my children were with me in the back of the Jeep. As we came to rest upside down by a stream, my first thought was, "Are they still alive?" I scrambled to crawl out and get back to them. They were both crying and the first intelligible words I heard were, "Boy, dad! Jesus really helped us." All three of us were trembling with shock, but thankfully unscathed. Ten or so Javanese villagers rolled our vehicle back over and we limped back home in our wrecked car. Bowen, Misi, and I must have said, "Boy, Jesus really did help us," a dozen times on our way back home.

I call this a *foxhole prayer*. They are spontaneous cries for God's help when we are in tough situations throughout the day. It may be a job interview, a pressing decision, or a phone call from someone needing our help. We feel a desperate need to call on God for wisdom, protection, guidance, or a miracle. I've found that He welcomes those cries for help.

Another kind of spontaneous prayer that erupts from my heart at times is a *prayer of intercession* for someone God brings to mind.

I am not naturally compassionate, so I've learned to recognize that familiar sense of God sharing with me His heart for someone. It seems so random at times. I'll be driving down the freeway or taking a shower when I feel stirred to pray for someone I may not have thought of in weeks or years. When I've had a dream about a particular individual I see this as a sign, an inspired prompting to pray for that person. Occasionally, a quickie prayer won't cut it. Waves of compassion may interrupt my schedule. There are times I have to pull over if I'm driving or pull out of a meeting and find a secluded spot and pray it through. As I write this, it's been six months since my wife and I led a medical relief team to North Sumatra in response to the devastating tsunamis. At times, faces of those who we treated still come to mind. A deep sadness or grief comes over me. I don't think I need a shrink. I just need to pray. I can't produce this spirit of intercession, but I've learned I need to respond to it.

There is growing popularity about the idea of *listening prayer*.[1] Some have asked why I don't include listening as a part of my daily prayer routine. The fact is God often gives each of us impressions, understanding and insight as we pray. He "speaks" through His word. I'd like to think I am listening throughout that hour or two that I spend seeking Him. But my experience is that I can't schedule when He speaks to me. I ask Him for direction often but rarely does He give me specific "words" when I am sitting in my living room or pacing on the back porch. He speaks at random times and in a variety of ways. My friend, Larry Kreider, has identified these many ways God speaks in his book *Hearing God: 30 Different Ways*. I recently went on a prayer retreat with the thought that I would focus on "praying through" some major decisions our church is facing regarding a new facility. I was an hour into this 48 hour retreat when I began to get some very clear direction on what I was to preach—my sermon series for the next six months! That's not what I was asking at that particular time, but the timing was perfect. I love when God does that! The directional word for the new facility came but not directly to me at that retreat. It came in bits and pieces in the weeks that followed through interaction with the staff and our building task force.

There is another kind of prayer I call *sitting in God's lap prayer.* Once again, we can't make this happen. But we can ask God for a fresh revelation of His fatherly, proactive, personal love for us. The Apostle Paul asked God to help us grasp how long, wide, high and deep His love for us—that we be rooted and grounded in that love.[2] This has happened to me at the most unpredictable times. One time that was particularly significant was on a Colorado ski trip with a couple of men from our church. One morning we were headed out to the slopes after breakfast, and I felt this strange desire to stay back in the room and prepare for a men's discipleship class I was creating at the time. (I say "strange" because I love to ski and I'm usually not responsible enough to prepare a teaching a week ahead of time.) To describe what happened next I must borrow the words of Charles Finney: "The Holy Spirit came upon me like waves of liquid love." I wept like a baby. At one point I could hardly stand. In the hour or so that followed I felt like scenes from my life were being flashed on the screen of my mind. Each chapter of my life was replayed with a running commentary that was repeated with each scene. I was taken back to my high school days in South Texas, then to my years in Austin where I attended college. There was a Los Angeles scene and a Houston scene. Then there were the three different cities where we had lived in Indonesia, and then back to Austin. Here was what the Holy Spirit repeated as each era was spotlighted: "Ron, you thought God had sent you to these different places to use you—to work through your life. But God's ultimate purpose was to show you more of His love for you in each of these seasons of your life." Words seem so inadequate to describe this revelation, but I am a different man because of it. You see why I wept? I was overwhelmed with a sense of God's love for *me*! That hour or so was worth more than 1,000 lift tickets.

Prayer Lab

1. Can you recall specific times in your spiritual journey when God showed you how much He loves you? Share one of those with a prayer partner or spouse (if you are married).

2. Turn Romans 5:5 and Ephesians 3:16-19 into personal prayers for God to show you His love in a fresh way.

Chapter 20

Fifteen Reasons to Set Aside Time to Pray Tomorrow

I challenge you to make an appointment with God sometime tomorrow. Most of you will find the best time to meet with Him is early in the morning, before your day cranks into gear. Whatever time works best for you make it a focused, intentional, proactive, pursuit of God's presence. If making and keeping this daily appointment becomes part of your life-style, routine and daily priority and you communicate with God in the ways I've suggested in this book, this is what will happen to you:

1. You will grow strong in Spirit
You will no longer be controlled by your old sin nature or your emotions, but you will walk in the Spirit.[1] You will find it easier to say *no* to ungodliness and worldly passions[2] and *yes* to God's will. You will find it easier to live out your true identity in Christ as one who is dead to the old way of living and alive in Christ.[3] Prayer leads to purity.

2. Because you pray, the other waking hours of your day will be more productive
When you "sacrifice" other activities in order to pray, you find the time you spend in prayer is no sacrifice at all. You seek first God's kingdom and everything else you need for a productive and meaningful life will be provided.[4]

3. You will experience more peace in your life

In prayer you will find it easier to turn over to God the stress points of your life. You won't be anxious about anything because you've turned those worries into specific prayers of petitions.[5] Your friends will comment on how less stressed-out you are compared to when you didn't pray.

4. You will sleep better

Not only will you carry things lighter throughout the day; but, when it comes time to sleep, you won't be harassed by those anxious thoughts. You will lay your head on your pillow with a clean conscience toward God and others.[6] When you do wake up in the middle of the night, it will be much easier to go back to sleep when you pray. (If it's the devil who is keeping you from sleeping, he will learn to let you sleep to keep you from praying more!)

5. Your relationships with others will be richer and more meaningful because you experience more of God's compassion for the people in your life for whom you pray

Whenever you wrong others you will more easily sense the conviction of the Holy Spirit.[7] Whenever they wrong you, you will be able to release their offense to God because you yourself have asked and received forgiveness so often in prayer.[8]

6. You will be more sensitive to the promptings, the nudges, and the guidance of the Holy Spirit throughout your day

There's an old hymn that says: "Turn your radio on and listen to the music in the air..." Prayer tunes your heart to have better reception to God's frequency—to His voice.

7. You will experience more of God's grace in your life

God resists the proud, but gives grace to the humble.[9] True prayer is an act of humility. We are declaring our total and utter dependence on God when we pray. Who doesn't want more of God's grace in their lives?

8. You will influence others in your life to want to pray more

Your roommates who love Jesus will want to follow your example. If you are married, and your spouse is a Christian, he or she will be inspired to *go for it* in prayer. If they are not yet believers, they will feel the conviction of the Holy Spirit. If you are a parent of children who are at home, you will model the most important behavior they could ever emulate.

9. You will get to know God better

You will cultivate true intimacy with the triune God through spending time with Him in prayer. It will not be a *head knowledge*, but rather a *heart knowledge*. You will learn of His ways—you will learn what pleases Him.[10] You will have a growing revelation of His character—His person. And this growing knowledge of Him will ignite greater passion to know Him more.[11]

10. You will learn how to better know the condition of your own heart

When you learn to pour out your heart to God in prayer, you have more self-awareness. True prayer is like a mirror of your soul. When you get real with God in your prayer journal and in prayer, without pretense or "posing," you will find it easier to let yourself be known by others (this is especially helpful for men).

11. You will better discern the difference between the condemning lies of our accuser, Satan, and the truth that God wants to communicate to you

Each time you declare the truth about what God says about you you grow in your ability to live out that identity in Christ.

12. You will change the world

Your prayers will affect the lives for whom you pray.[12] Your prayers advance God's purposes on the earth. Your prayers drive back the darkness. Your prayers transform you. God's power is more clearly demonstrated through your prayers.[13]

13. You will love God

Prayer is the most direct, tangible way we can express our love to God. Something in us comes alive when we love God with unabashed adornment; we were created to love Him. More significantly, we actually warm His heart through our words of adoration, thanksgiving, and trust.

14. You experience more of His personal love for you

I heard someone say recently, "I pray every morning because I don't want to face my day without being reminded of how much God loves me." Prayer is your opportunity to experience God's kind, fatherly, proactive, unconditional, and transforming love for you. He delights in pouring out His love into your heart through His Holy Spirit.[14] He does that when we make room in our schedules through daily prayer.

15. You bring greater glory to God. When we pray we are declaring...

...His incomparable worth. You honor and revere Him when you give up time you could be sleeping, watching television, listening to a radio talk show or reading the newspaper in order to meet with Him. We bring Him glory through every kind of prayer, even prayers in which we are asking Him for things. [15]

Why is it so important to begin to pray tomorrow? It is because tomorrow's action will affect the rest of your life: "Sow an action; reap a habit. Sow a habit; reap a character. Sow a character; reap a destiny." If tomorrow's prayer time is repeated the next day and the next, it will eventually become a habit. You will become like Jesus who *as was His custom often withdrew to lonely places and prayed.*[16]

I knew of a young man in his early twenties who began to pray an hour or so every day. There were days he missed his appointment with God, but His passion to pray increased over time. So his time with God became more consistent. It also became more life-giving, more fulfilling. He actually began to enjoy prayer more than anything else in his life. The more he prayed, the more he wanted to pray. Nearly thirty years later, that guy is a middle-aged pastor wanting to convince everyone he knows that they can learn to delight in prayer.

Endnotes

Introduction
[1] 1 Timothy 4:7-8 NLT

[2] Ephesians 6:18

Chapter 1
[1] Luke 5:15-16

[2] John 5:19

[3] John 8:28

[4] Mother Teresa, *No Greater Love*, p. 8

[5] Ephesians 6:18

[6] 1 Thessalonians 5:17

[7] Hebrews 5:11 NLT

[8] John 11:41-42 NLT

[9] James 5:16

[10] Matthew 16:19

[11] Exodus 33-34

[12] Acts 12:5

[13] James 5:16

[14] John 14:13-14

Chapter 2
[1] Psalm 16:11

[2] Song of Solomon 1:2

[3] John 14:27

[4] Mark 1:11

[5] John 17:26, 15:9

[6] Zephaniah 3:17

[7] Romans 5:5

[8] Ephesians 3:16-18

Chapter 3
[1] Acts 2:42

[2] Colossians 4:2

[3] 1 Thessalonians 5:17

[4] 1 Peter 5:7

[5] Ephesians 3:17-19

[6] Hebrews 10:24

Chapter 4
[1] Matthew 6:6

[2] Luke 5:16

[3] Daniel 6:10-12

[4] Acts 4:24

Chapter 6
[1] Ephesians 6:18a

Chapter 7
[1] Psalm 100:4

[2] Hebrews 12:28 NLT

[3] Luke 17:15-16

Chapter 8
[1] 2 Chronicles 20:5-7

[2] Luke 11:2

[3] *Eerdman's Handbook to the History of Christianity,* pp. 442-444

Chapter 9
[1] Acts 24:16

[2] Isaiah 6:1-5

[3] Psalm 51:6

[4] John 16:8

[5] Psalm 139:23-24 NLT

[6] Psalm 51:1

[7] 1 John 1:9

Chapter 10
[1] James 4:7

[2] Luke 22:42

[3] John 6:38 NLT

[4] Romans 12:1

[5] 1 Corinthians 6:20

[6] 1 Timothy 6:19

Chapter 11
[1] Ephesians 6:18

[2] Philippians 4:6 NLT

[3] Luke 11:8

[4] 1 Timothy 2:9

[5] Luke 22:42

[6] James 4:3

[7] Luke 18:4

[8] Luke 18:1

[9] Mark 10:51a

[10] Mark 10:51b

[11] John 15:7-8

[12] James 4:2

[13] Jim Collins, *Built to Last*

[14] Acts 4:30

Chapter 12
[1] Luke 22:42

[2] Luke 13:34

[3] Psalm 13:1-2

[4] Psalm 22:1-2

[5] Psalm 142:2)

[6] Psalm 74:1, 9, 12-13 NLT

[7] John 21:6

[8] 2 Kings 20:1-7

Chapter 13

1 Psalm 68:5

2 Psalm 10:14

3 Philippians 4:19

4 Psalm 57:2-3 NLT

5 Psalm 56:4 NLT

6 Daniel 9:4 NLT

7 Psalm 57:7 NLT

Chapter 14

1 2 Corinthians 10:4 NLT

2 Matthew 6:10

3 1 Timothy 6:12

4 Matthew 28:18

5 Mark 16:16-18

6 Matthew 16:19

7 Ephesians 6:12

8 Ephesians 6:18

9 *Let the Nations Be Glad*, by John Piper, p. 49

10 Matthew 4:4-11

11 Ephesians 6:17

12 John Eldredge, *Waking the Dead*, pp. 178-179

Chapter 15

1 Jeremiah 32:16-19 - NLT

2 Ephesians 1:16-19

3 Ephesians 3:16-19

Chapter 17

1 1 Corinthians 14:14

2 1 Corinthians 14:2

3 1 Corinthians 14:4

4 1 Corinthians 14:18

5 1 Corinthians 14:15

6 1 Corinthians 14:14

7 1 Corinthians 14:16

8 1 Corinthians 10:5

9 1 Corinthians 14:2

10 Acts 2:11

11 1 Corinthians 14:16

12 Romans 8:26

13 1 Corinthians 14:4

14 1 Corinthians 12:30

15 1 Corinthians 14:1

16 David Barrett's research on the status of Christianity in the world reflects that the fast growing segment of Christianity in many non-western countries is the Pentecostal/Charismatic/Third Wave churches who practice glossolalia.

Chapter 19

1 For example LeeAnn Payne's book, *Listening Prayer*

2 Ephesians 3:18-19

Chapter 20

1 Romans 8:2

2 Titus 2:12

3 Romans 6:1-4

4 Matthew 6:33

5 Philippians 4:6-7

6 Acts 24:16

7 Matthew 5:23-24

8 Matthew 6:14; 18:21-35

9 1 Peter 5:5

10 Colossians 1:10

11 Philippians 3:10

12 James 5:16

13 John 14:13-14

14 Romans 5:5

15 John 14:12-14

16 Luke 5:16

Small Group Discussion Guide

Discussion Leader: Each chapter will have more discussion questions than you can possibly cover in an hour. You'll need to pick and choose which ones will be most relevant to your group. Make sure you leave time for the last question since it is designed to lead into life application and prayer.

You have the ability to set the tone of this discussion by being real and vulnerable with those in your group. Share freely your own struggles and others will be open about theirs. Do your best to keep it *grace-filled*. Avoid condemning those who struggle with prayerlessness.

Motivations: Desperation and Expectation

1. If you were to give your prayer life a grade right now, what would your report card look like?
   Time spent in focused interaction with God _____
   Consistency to pray daily _____
   Experiencing God's presence when you pray _____
   Prayer is really fun for you _____

2. What are some motivations to pray that haven't worked for you? Guilt? Obligation? A fear of something bad happening to you if you don't pray more? A need to make up for some ways you've blown it with God?

3. Have you ever made a commitment to pray more and not followed through on that commitment? Why?

   Read Luke 5:15-16.

4. How would you describe Jesus' prayer life?

5. What activities or "busyness" did Jesus pull away from in order to be alone with God, His Father? How does the demands of Jesus' schedule compare with the challenges of your schedule that keep you from praying more?

6. How important do you think it is to have healthy motivations to experience a meaningful, consistent time of daily prayer?

7. In this chapter the author mentions two motivations that caused Jesus to withdraw from the demands on his life and pray. What are your thoughts?
Do you think Jesus was really desperate to meet with God?
How confident do you think Jesus was that His prayers were making a difference?

Discussion Leader: Have each person share a sincere prayer like: Heavenly Father, I really desire that my times spent with You_____.
Then have each person pray for someone else in the group— praying especially for their devotional life.

Motivations: Delight and Awareness

1. Describe something silly or embarrassing that you've done to get some time with someone you are (were) really close to.

Discussion Leader: Share one of your more embarrassing moments when you were dating, like sneaking out of your house at night to meet your boyfriend or girlfriend.

2. How do you think the "love-motive" factored into Jesus' lifestyle of consistently finding time to be alone with God, His Father? (Luke 5:15-16)

3. Mother Teresa said: "Prayer to Him (God) is loving Him." Do you agree/disagree? Why?

4. How would it affect your prayer life if you were more passionately in love with Jesus Christ?

5. Read Ephesians 3:16-18. How important is it for us to experience God's personal love for us? Why/why not?

6. Share a time that you realized that God loved *you*.

Discussion Leader: Be sensitive to those in your group who share that they have never experienced God's personal love for them. It's an excellent opportunity for the group to pray for each other.

7. How do you think it would change your prayer life if you really believed that "God was eager to meet with you...waiting next to your bed...anticipating the moment you open your eyes."

Discussion Leader: Give opportunities for each person to turn some of their desires into heartfelt prayers.

Making Time for Prayer

1. Describe what it would look like for a man to be "devoted" to his work.
   What about someone "devoted" to sports or *devoted* to ones family?
   What do you think he meant when Paul said we were to be *devoted* to prayer (Colossians 4:2)?

2. What do you say to someone who says: "I really don't need to set aside time to pray every day. I pray throughout the day"? What did the author say to challenge this idea?

3. What are some examples from the Bible that come to mind of the value of *going for it in prayer* daily?

4. How do you turn a *desire* to want to pray more into *delighting* in prayer?

5. What are your thoughts about this statement: "The key to becoming *consistent* in prayer is to be *persistent* in prayer"?

6. How does it feel to you to think that you can keep starting over in prayer when you've missed a day or two (or more)?

7. What are some practical ways Ron mentions that could help someone begin to be more discipline to pray?

8. What do you intend to do—what would help you grow in this discipline?

Discussion Leader: Ask each person responding to this question something like, "When we get together next, do we have permission to ask you whether you have made progress or not?"

Discover Your Prayer Style

Discussion Leader: Go around the room and ask how each person has applied what they have learned or how they have begun to live out the strategies we talked about last week to grow in the discipline of prayer.

1. What are some prayer styles that you've heard (or ways people have prayed) that have struck you as funny?

Discussion Leader: Avoid people in the group making fun of the prayer idiosyncrasies of others in the group! The danger of this question is that people might get their feelings hurt unless they are really secure in their relationships.

2. Why is it important to pray alone? Can you think of any examples or statements from scripture that may reinforce this practice?

3. Where is (or has been) your favorite place to pray (even if it is a place far from where you live now)?

4. Why does the author suggest praying out loud?
   What are your thoughts?

5. What's your favorite praying posture?
   Which one would be new for you?
   Which would you like to try?

6. What from this chapter encouraged or challenged you?
   What do you intend to do about it?

Keeping a Prayer Journal

1. What has been one of your most exciting and undeniable answers to prayer?

2. Do you think there may have been prayers you've prayed and God has answered, that you've forgotten?
How would this reality motivate individuals to record their prayers?

3. What would be some other benefits to keeping a prayer journal?

4. Have you found journaling your prayers helpful? Share what you've learned about journaling that may help others in the group.

5. What are some practical things about keeping a prayer journal that you've learned from this chapter?

6. Write a letter to God this week. Pour out your heart to Him. Tell Him your joys, fears, your longings and burdens. Bring it to the group next week and share the parts of your letter you are comfortable sharing.

All Kinds of Prayers

1. Be honest, have you ever found prayer to be rather boring? Have you ever fallen asleep while praying?

   Read Ephesians 6:18

2. What are some *kinds of prayers* that come to mind for you?

3. What are some suggestions the author makes in this chapter that might keep your prayer times fresh and vibrant?

4. What is a "prayer pattern" that you've used?
   What's been good about it? What has not worked for you?

5. From your perspective what would be the benefit to praying according to a specific outline every day?
   Potential downsides?

Discussion Leader: Close the discussion by having the group pray together according the ACTS or Lord's Prayer Outline.

Prayers of Gratitude and Thanksgiving

1. Can you think of a time recently when someone went out of their way to express appreciation to you? How did you feel?

2. Find some verses in the Bible that speak of how important it is for us to learn to express our gratitude to God. Read them out loud as a group.

3. **Discussion Leader:** Have a concordance or two handy for this exercise.

4. What do you think it means to *overflow with gratitude*? What if you don't *feel* grateful?

5. Does it seem insincere to you to "choose" to express thanks to God when you don't necessarily feel it?

6. What are some specific ways the author suggested that could help you cultivate prayers of gratitude during your prayer times?

Discussion Leader: Have each of the group members make a "thankful list." Give them 7–10 minutes to work alone. Then, have them take turns and pray several of the items on their list. An alternative would be to have everyone pray their lists out loud all at once. You could also have people pair off and share a couple of items with their list and rejoice together in prayer.

Chapter 8

Prayers of Adoration and Praise

1. What's currently one of your favorite worship songs? If you had to pick one, which would be your all-time-favorite worship song? Now sing it to the group. (Just kidding!)

Discussion Leader: Try the experiment Ron suggested at the beginning of this chapter. Have everyone limit their prayers to just prayers of adoration and praise for the next 10 minutes.

2. Was it difficult not to launch into prayers of petition/request? Why/why not?

3. Try to find a prayer in the Bible that doesn't start with acknowledging the person or character of God (adoration)? Read several out loud that begin with adoration or praise.

4. The author suggests several practical ways to worship God in your times of personal devotion. Which of these is new to you?

5. Would you be willing to try out one of these ways of engaging your heart in adoration and praise in your prayer times this week? Would you be open to sharing what you experienced in praying this week the next time we come together?

Prayers of Confession and Repentance

Discussion Leader: Remind the group of their commitment to pray prayers of adoration and praise last week. Have people share what they experienced.

1. Share a time the Holy Spirit convicted you of a specific sin and you knew you needed to confess it to God (and others). How did it feel when you obeyed?

2. Describe the difference between confession and repentance.

3. How are some ways we could *not* respond to the voice of the Holy Spirit when He is showing us how we've blown it? Have you ever tried one of these ways?

4. Read Psalm 51 and 1 John 1:8-2:2. What can we learn about confession of sin from these verses?

5. How does the author suggest "one distinguish between the conviction of the Holy Spirit and the condemning lies of our accuser—Satan?"

6. What if you start to pray and nothing comes to mind for which you need to repent?

Discussion Leader: If your group is larger than 6 people divide into groups of 4 or less. It's best to have smaller groups of the same gender. Have groups read Psalm 139:23-24, then wait on the Lord for 5 minutes or so. Pray prayers of confession and repentance as the Holy Spirit brings things to mind. Have others speak Christ's forgiveness to those who are repenting.

Chapter 10 Discussion Guide

Prayers of Submission and Surrender

1. What's something that was really of great value to you that you freely surrendered to God?
   How did you come to the decision to sacrifice in this way?

2. What are some Bible verses that come to mind (or that the author refers to in this chapter) that speak of how we are to surrender everything to God?

3. What are the promises that God makes to us as a result of our willingness to sacrifice?

4. We surrendered our rights, even our lives to Christ when we became Christians.
   How come the author suggests we need to do so repeatedly?

5. Share a time that you needed to once again submit to Christ's lordship in your life. (Can you think of a recent occasion?)

6. What do you think of this statement: "There is no greater joy than in total surrender."

7. Of all the areas of your life, what do you find the most challenging to fully surrender to God right now?
   Would you be willing to pray a prayer from your heart giving this to God right here?

Discussion Leader: Lead the group in prayers of surrender. If the group is larger than six, divide the group up into groups of four or less for prayer.

Chapter 11 Discussion Guide

Prayers of Request and Bold Petition

1. When you have a need are you typically shy or reluctant to trouble others or are you the type of person who is free to ask people to go out of their way to help you. Give an example.

   Read Luke 11:5-8.

2. What was the key to the man receiving what he needed? What does Jesus seem to be teaching us about prayer?

3. According to the author what does it mean to pray *with gall*?

4. What did the author mean by *God's Will-Phobia*? Have you ever suffered from this malady?

5. What biblical basis is there for continuing to ask God for something you've yet to receive?

6. Is there something you've given up asking God for because it has seemed it's never going to happen?

7. Is there something you've wanted to ask God for, but have been reluctant to ask?

8. Do you have your own B.H.A.P.?

Discussion Leader: Provide an opportunity for people to write down and/or pray their answers to questions 6-8.

Prayers of Lament

1. What would you say to a 6-year-old who shares with you that she asked God for a puppy and God didn't answer her prayer.

2. What is a prayer of lament? Read some examples from the Word.

3. Have you ever asked God for something that you really wanted, only to be disappointed that it never happened? Are you free to share it with us?

4. How have you responded to the disappointment of unanswered prayer?

5. What are some thoughts or ideas about healthy lamenting that were new or helpful to you?

6. What are some ways that you may be grieving, disappointed, or even angry at God right now? Are you willing to share it with us and give us an opportunity to lament with you?

Discussion Leader: What a great opportunity to minister to each other!

Prayers of Trust

1. What does it do to you when your boss, your spouse, your parent, or one of your friends expresses trust in you?

2. How does this apply to our relationship with God?

3. The author states: "You may feel a deep level trust in God but that trust needs to be expressed and communicated." How do we communicate our trust in God? What are some examples from the Bible?

4. Are you ever harassed by condemning lies from our enemy, Satan? What are some of the lies that Satan tries to make you believe?

Discussion Leader: If your group is vulnerable enough to share on this level then give others in the group a chance to counter those lies by speaking God's *truth* in response to what they are hearing.

5. Look at Ron's list of statements of "Who God says I am." What would it look like if you began to believe this about yourself? What if you turned this list into "prayer declarations" on a regular basis?

Discussion Leader: An alternative to the above exercise would be to use Ron's list as a prompt to get the group praying prayers declaring who we are because of Christ.

Chapter 14

Kingdom Warfare Prayers

1. When you were a kid did you ever get in a fight with the neighborhood bully? (Perhaps *you* were the neighborhood bully!)

2. In your opinion, how is prayer sometimes like a battle?

3. According to the author what are some characteristics of Kingdom Warfare Prayer?

4. What would be some consequences of a Christian never learning to pray this way?

5. On a scale of 1-10 how often do you exercise the authority God has given us to defeat our enemy through spiritual warfare? How do you think God wants you to grow in this area?

Discussion Leader: Have the group turn their longings into prayers.

6. Personalize John Eldredge's prayer the author quotes from *Raising the Dead* by praying it out loud.

Praying the Bible

1. If you've been a Christian for a while, you've probably used some of your favorite verses from the Bible in your prayers. Quote (or read) some of you all-time favorites.

Discussion Leader: One alternative to the above questions would be to have the members of the group pray those verses.

2. What are some advantages to incorporating the Bible into your prayers?

3. What are some ways the author suggests you could take what you are reading in the Word and turn it into powerful prayers?

Discussion Leader: Have one person pick any chapter in the Bible. (They will probably pick some obscure chapter in the Old Testament) Then go around the room and have each person form a short prayer from this chapter. Remind them it could be prayers other than prayers of petition.

4. What would it take for you to pray this way beginning in Genesis and working your way all the way to the end of Revelation? Why wouldn't you want to try?

Prayers Worth Repeating

1. What's the funniest prayer you ever heard someone pray?
   How about the most inspiring?

2. What's a "borrowed" prayer?
   Have you ever prayed this kind of prayer?
   Where (besides the Bible) have you found these kinds of prayers?

3. What are the steps to composing a crafted prayer?

4. If you were to write out a crafted prayer, what would be the topic (i.e. freedom, boldness, joy, love, authority, etc.)?

5. What's one idea from this chapter that was inspiring to you?
   What are you going to do about it?

Discussion Leader: Have the people in your group make a first run at writing out a crafted prayer for the meeting next week.

Praying With Our Spirit

1. What was your reaction when you first heard someone praying in tongues?

2. Is the idea of praying in tongues new to you? If you've experienced this type of prayer, have you found it helpful? Explain.

   Read 1 Corinthians 14:2-5.

3. What does Paul say about tongues here? Why did Paul say he would like every one of the Corinthians to speak in tongues?

4. Why do you think Paul says later on in this chapter: *I thank God I speak in tongues more than you all* ? (1 Corinthians 14:18) Why did he pray and sing *with his spirit* (verse 15)?

5. Why did the author say that for Paul, prayer in the Spirit took place in his private prayer times, not in the worship gatherings? (verse 19)

6. Why are some people afraid of speaking in tongues?

7. Why does the author say that *ecstatic utterance* is a poor translation of the Greek word *glossolalia*?

Discussion Leader: Ask if individuals in the group would like to experience the gift of tongues. Be prepared to pray with those who are seeking this gift or refer them to someone you know who is familiar with this gift.

A Life-Giving Hour Spent with God

1. Do you see yourself as a scheduled-routine type of person or are you more spontaneous?
Share an example.

Discussion Leader: Ask if anyone in the group could list the progression or kinds of prayers the author suggests in this chapter for an hour of life-giving prayer?

2. How would see your personality fitting with the kind of prayer format the author suggests in this chapter?
If you are more spontaneous, does this feel too restricting? Explain.

3. Be honest. How would you feel if one day you would get "stuck" just praying prayers of adoration or thanksgiving?
Are you okay with *not* completing the list?
What are the authors thoughts about this?

4. When Ron says: *I'm never bound to a rigid set of prayers...The fact is: no two prayer times are alike.*
Is this your experience in prayer? Explain.

5. What's one idea from this chapter that you would really like to apply tomorrow?

Unscheduled Prayers

1. Share a time recently when you prayed a prayer of desperation—*a foxhole prayer.*

2. What does the author mean by "unscheduled prayers"?

3. Can you recall a time recently when the Holy Spirit started speaking to you about something, out of the blue? Share it.

4. Why does the author contend that we can't really schedule times when God would speak to us or a spirit of intercession would come over us?
   Do you agree or disagree? Why?

5. What is a "sitting in God's lap" prayer?
   Have you ever experienced an overwhelming sense of God's fatherly, personal, proactive, kind, unconditional love for you? Share it with the group.

   Read Ephesians 3:14-19.

6. Personalize this prayer and pray it out loud for you, and your friends gathered for this small group.

Fifteen Reasons to Set Aside Time to Pray

1. Can you give a personal example of how you've experienced one of these benefits to spending time with God?

2. Which of these fifteen reasons motivates you most to want to carve out more time for prayer? Why?

3. Which of the 20 chapters of this book was the most inspiring to you?

4. What's one idea that you've gleaned from this book that has been most helpful to you?

5. Since you've begun reading this book what about your prayer life has changed? How have you grown?

6. Share with the group a new commitment you have to making your prayer times more life-giving.

Pray for each other.

For more examples

To see other examples of prayer journal entries, crafted prayers, and ways to pray the Word visit **www.hopeinthecity.org** and then go to Ron's Prayer Journal.

To contact the author

Email: delightingingprayer@hopeinthecity.org

To order additional copies

For more copies of *From Duty to Delight: Finding Greater Joy in Daily Prayer*

Call Hope in the City (512) 892-4673

Go to our web site www.hopeinthecity.org

and follow the link to *From Duty to Delight* Book Orders.

Quantity discounts available.